WILD PALMS

WILD PALMS

Bruce Wagner

St. Martin's Press
New York

Library of Congress Cataloging-in-Publication Data

Wagner, Bruce.
    Wild palms: the screenplay/Bruce Wagner; foreword by William Gibson.
            p.   cm.
    "A Thomas Dunne book."
    ISBN 0-312-10616-5
    I. Title.
PS3573.A369W55   1994
791.45'72—dc20   93-35848
                                                    CIP

First edition: January 1994

10 9 8 7 6 5 4 3 2 1

The wind is old and still at play
While I must hurry upon my way,
For I am running to Paradise . . .

WILD PALMS

Starring:

James Belushi
Dana Delany
Robert Loggia
Kim Cattrall
Angie Dickinson
Ernie Hudson

Also Starring:
Bebe Neuwirth
Nick Mancuso
Charles Hallahan
Robert Morse
David Warner
Ben Savage
Bob Gunton
and Brad Dourif as "Chickie Levitt"

Production Manager   Patti Kent
Production Design   Dins Danielsen
Costumes   Judianna Makovsky
Supervising Editor   Patrick McMahon
Executive Consultant   Roger Trilling
Casting   Rik Pagano, Sharon Bialy, Debi Manwiller
Visual Effects   Pacific Data Images
Director of Photography   Phedon Papamichail
Music   Ryuichi Sakamoto
Producer   Michael Rauch
Writer and Creator   Bruce Wagner
Executive Producers   Bruce Wagner and Oliver Stone

Special Thanks To: Tony Krantz and the Babies, James Truman, Julian Allen, Alex Ho, John and Nancy at Digital, Zaia, Stu Sweeney, Janine C., Annie Riccitelli,
and all the boys at ABC (you know who you are)

"Everything Must Go" directed by Peter Hewitt
"The Floating World" directed by Keith Gordon
"Rising Sons" directed by Kathryn Bigelow
"Hungry Ghosts" directed by Keith Gordon
"Hello, I Must Be Going" directed by Phil Joanou

Foreword

Bruce Wagner wrote these scripts in the Chateau Marmont, a structure already skewed somewhat sideways to the common time line. He worked in a series of suites, moving each time the accumulated "bad energies" built up to what he rightly sensed were *dangerously* toxic levels. Wagner is someone who understands these things, I believe, and not entirely at any merely *conscious* level. My feeling at the time was that Wagner was handling dangerous materials up there in the Marmont; that he was, in fact, using that whole benevolently haunted, rococo concrete folly as a type of giant *waldo*—one of those skeletal alloy hands employed in the handling of intensely hazardous substances.

This impression was only heightened by my one visit with him there, as the actual production got underway.

Wagner, the only man I've ever known who uses the kind of shaver that leaves a perfect, three-day stubble, was wrapped in a capacious white, terrycloth robe. The living room of the suite was filled with books, though I felt intuitively that their presence had more to do with some sort of cabalistic operation than with any more mundane employment. They were arranged, face up, on every available surface, and I sensed that the very manner of their arrangement had to do with the dissipation of "bad energies."

In the adjoining dining area, atop a faux-Mission oak table, the screen of a carbon-gray laptop gave off an umber glow.

I don't recall exactly what it was that we *spoke* of, but I do recall the eerie feeling that Wagner was *listening,* constantly, as if for some telltale sound—*something slightly beyond the ordinary range of human hearing.*

In light of the subsequent political history of the United States, I have come to the conclusion that Wagner was actually engaged, then and there, in an unconscious magical operation of quite an unthinkable scope.

The act of writing these scripts prevented the reelection of George Bush.

William Gibson, Vancouver, 8/9/93

WILD PALMS

"Everything Must Go"

ACT ONE

FADE IN:

EXT. RESIDENTIAL STREET—CLOSE—PALM—NIGHT

It FILLS the FRAME. FRONDS SCRAPE and shimmer against each other in the WIND, foreboding and electric, unsettling.

ROW OF PALM TREES

the roaring, scary WINDSONG.

SWIMMING POOL

The dark trees reflected within its waters.

INT. WYCKOFF HOUSE—MASTER BEDROOM—NIGHT

HARRY'S eyes open; perspiring and insomniac. The palms are calling him. He gets up from bed; GRACE doesn't awaken. Harry slides open glass door of patio. Wind ruffles his hair.

EXT. WYCKOFF HOUSE—BACK YARD—NIGHT

Poolside. The palms' noisy, full-tilt war against the wind. Harry proceeds cautiously.

A rhinoceros stands in the shallow end of pool. The waters around it are choppy like the sea.

CLOSE—RHINO'S HORN

CLOSE—HARRY

He watches, mesmerized. A hoarse whisper:

> HARRY
> So, this is how it begins. . . .

> COTY (V.O.)
> Daddy?

He runs toward house, to voice.

INT. WYCKOFF HOUSE—COTY'S ROOM—NIGHT

Harry enters breathlessly. What he sees staggers him: COTY is suspended on an enormous crucifix in the middle of the furnitureless room. He wears a black Chanel T-shirt and smiles wickedly while he hovers—and sadly sings:

(CONTINUED)

                          COTY
Never saw the sun shinin' so bright . . . never saw
love feelin' so right . . . Blue skies—

INT. WYCKOFF HOUSE—MASTER BEDROOM—NIGHT

Harry awakens with a sweaty jolt from his dream.

                          GRACE
                       (concerned)
        Darling?

EXT. WYCKOFF HOUSE—MORNING

A Wagoneer and a couple of 60's cars—including Harry's
Corvette—in the drive of the Spanish-style home. A light wind; a
subdued row of palms, not up to last night's excitations.

INT. WYCKOFF HOUSE—KITCHEN—MORNING

A stylish cappuccino maker. Grace injects steam, foaming up the
milk. She brings it to Harry, who sits in a black leather banquette;
settles in beside him.

                          HARRY
        Is that decaf?

                          GRACE
        Did you want decaf, darling?

                          HARRY
        No, I'm fine. Hmmm—good foam. You've got a
        real skill there.

                          GRACE
        You know I'm a damn household goddess, Harry.
        Bagel's on the way.

                          HARRY
        What a night.

                          GRACE
        Remember your dream?

                          HARRY
        It was weird—I remember that much.

                          GRACE
        You scared the hell out of me.

                          HARRY
        Where are the kids?

                                                    (CONTINUED)

                              GRACE
              Little Buddha's getting her bath. I think Coty's got
              a bug, so I'm keeping him home.

                              HARRY
              Why do bugs love that kid so much?

                              GRACE
              'Cause he's so juicy. He had a call-back for a
              toothpaste commercial.

                              HARRY
              Should we have his tum-tum checked?

                              GRACE
              He just has a nervous stomach—like his old man.

                              HARRY
              Waitress? I think my bagel is burning.

Grace shrieks, retrieves smoking bagel from toaster.

                              GRACE
              It's sort of charred.

                              HARRY
              I like it that way.

                              GRACE
              I'll put another one in.

                              HARRY
              I said bring it here, woman.

                              GRACE
              Such a nasty man . . .

TAMBOR, the nanny, enters, holding Deirdre—swathed in towels.
Grace takes Deirdre in her arms and baby-talks.

                              GRACE
              There she is! Dere's duh wet wittle Buddha!

                              HARRY
              I'm gonna look in on the stomach-acher. We still
              have a date tonight?

                              GRACE
              Uh huh. The kids are staying with Josie.

                              HARRY
              How's her face?

> GRACE
> Thoroughly lifted.

> HARRY
> (kissing Deirdre)
> Morning, little Buddha. You are one helluva
> gorgeous old soul. Ol' King Cole was a scary Ol'
> Soul, and a scary Ol' Soul was she . . .

COTY'S BEDROOM—CLOSE ON TV SCREEN

A Sesame Street-style character waves good-bye to the camera as the
WPN/CHANNEL THREE logo is SUPERED.

Harry enters, turns OFF TV. Coty is asleep. He tucks covers under his
son.

> COTY
> (groggily)
> I have a bug.

> HARRY
> Well, you gotta scare that bug away, Mr. Blue.

> COTY
> (rolling over to sleep)
> Love you, Daddy.

Harry smiles, kisses him; exits. As soon as he leaves, Coty's eyes
open. We HOLD ON them a beat.

EXT. STREETS—MORNING

Harry cruises in his Corvette. He slows; sees two Men in Suits
beating a third man. He moves on.

A motorcycle cop appears, making way for motorcade: black Range
Rovers, along with other unmarked vehicles, move slowly alongside
white-haired jogger in his early sixties—SENATOR ANTON "TONY"
KREUTZER. He's surrounded by other joggers, obviously security.
Kreutzer turns to glance at Harry, his gaze prolonged and strangely
deliberate; then, the party disappears over a ridge. Harry shrugs it off
and pulls onto road again.

INT. BAUM, WEISS AND LATIMER—OFFICE/ANTEROOM—DAY

Art Moderne decor. Harry enters office; PAULA, his assistant, greets
him. She's in her 20s, wears a 50's "poodle skirt."

> PAULA
> Hi, Harry.

> HARRY
> Groovy dress.

(CONTINUED)

                    PAULA
                    (nods)
Got it at your wife's store.

                    HARRY
Things are just getting too incestuous: Paula,
you're fired.

                    PAULA
                    (laughs)
I forgot to tell you—my kid's in a play today. I
have to leave at four—

                    HARRY
Go ahead, abandon me. What am I doing for
lunch?

MORTY WINAKUR, a fellow attorney, enters. He's balding, in his
40s: smarmy-looking, but affable.

                    MORTY
Hey, Jude.

                    PAULA
You have a one o'clock with Mr. Laszlo, at City.

                    HARRY
Is that Third or Sixth?

                PAULA AND MORTY
La Brea and Second.

                    MORTY
                    (to Harry)
So, when's the special day?

                    HARRY
                    (to Paula)
Morty and I are getting married.

                    MORTY
Come on—everybody knows you're making
partner.

                    HARRY
Rumor, Morty.

                    MORTY
You're so coy.

                    PAULA
Paige Katz is here.

(CONTINUED)

                              HARRY
            Great. Send her in.

                              MORTY
            Who's Paige Katz?

                              HARRY
            Bye, Morty—

                              MORTY
            Did I tell you Ann was pregnant again?

                              HARRY
                              (sincere)
            That's terrific.

                              MORTY
            A little girl. She's always talking about <u>bloat,</u> so I
            told her to start telling people she's 'retaining
            daughter.'
                              (laughs)
            Do you love it?

                              HARRY
            Love it.

                              MORTY
            Catch ya later—<u>partner.</u>

                              HARRY
            This is going to be a weird day.

Paula escorts PAIGE KATZ into the office, then exits shutting door.
Paige carries small portfolio; they kiss. They both seem a little
nervous.

                              PAIGE
            I felt funny calling.

                              HARRY
            No, no—it was great to hear from you.

They sit on the couch.

                              HARRY
            Would you like a cappuccino? Some Evian?

                              PAIGE
            No. Thanks.

                              HARRY
            It <u>was</u> pretty out of the blue. . . .

                              PAIGE
            A blast from the past.

                                              (CONTINUED)

                    HARRY
How long has it been?

                    PAIGE
Fifteen years?
                    (notes ring)
You're married—naturally.

                    HARRY
Yes.

                    PAIGE
Happily?

                    HARRY
Naturally.

                    PAIGE
Kids?

                    HARRY
Two. You?

                    PAIGE
I have a son—out of wedlock.

                    HARRY
Are you working?

                    PAIGE
I'm a consultant for the Wild Palms Group. Two
kids, huh. I always knew you were daddy
material.

                    HARRY
There was something you wanted to talk to me
about. . . .

                    PAIGE
I want you to help me find someone.

                    HARRY
That's a little Raymond Chandler, Paige. I'm a
patent attorney. . . .

                    PAIGE
It's my son Peter. He disappeared five years
ago. . . .

INT. HIROSHIMA—DAY

Grace's retro-eclectic Melrose boutique. She enters from back room,
greeting OAKLEY, a frantic salesgirl in zoot suit. Oakley finishes with
a customer, who exits.

(CONTINUED)

> GRACE
> Hey, Oakley. What's happening?

> OAKLEY
> Your mom just called.

> GRACE
> (remembering)
> No! I'm supposed to pick her up. Why am I doing
> this, Oakley? I'm an adult woman, I have a
> life—why am I compelled to pick my mother up
> at the hospital after her fifty-seventh face-lift?

> OAKLEY
> Do you want me to answer that?

> GRACE
> Not really.

Grace sees the glamorous TABBA SCHWARTZKOPF staring into
window; Tabba carries about seven bags from different stores.

> GRACE
> Is that Tabba Schwartzkopf?

> OAKLEY
> The actress?

> GRACE
> (excited)
> It is. She's coming in.

Tabba enters.

> OAKLEY
> Easy, Grace.

> GRACE
> Did you see her in Magnificent Obsession?

> OAKLEY
> Wasn't that like the tenth time they made that?

> GRACE
> She was so great. . . .

> TABBA
> Hi! I need to ask you something that will probably
> arouse a kind of sickening contempt.

> GRACE
> You need to use the phone.

(CONTINUED)

                          TABBA
Worse. The bathroom.

                          GRACE
Oh, no!

                          TABBA
                          (laughs)
I'm a terrible person.

                          GRACE
But you break just like a little girl.
                    (as Tabba cracks up)
Oakley, please show Miss Schwartzkopf the
communal loo.

                          TABBA
                       (mock shame)
She even knows my name—it's so sad.

                          GRACE
                          (a fan)
I've seen all your movies.

                          TABBA
I've used all your bathrooms.

They laugh.

EXT. THE BEVERLY CLINIC—DAY

Grace gets out of car as her mother, JOSIE, exits building in
wheelchair, pushed by NURSE. Josie's dressed in a Chanel suit; any
scars from facial surgery are invisible.

                          GRACE
                       (kissing her)
You look <u>fabulous.</u>

                          NURSE
                    (overly enthused)
Doesn't she?

                          JOSIE
Never again. It <u>hurt</u> this time.

                          GRACE
They did a <u>terrific</u> job—

                          JOSIE
Good-bye, Cruella—
          (to Grace, re: Nurse, affectionately)
That's Cruella de Vil.

                                              (CONTINUED)

                              GRACE
          I'm Grace—the daughter.
                    (helps Josie into car)
          Was she a horror?

                              NURSE
                    (shakes head)
          A <u>delight.</u>

                              JOSIE
          They'll say anything—they're so <u>thrilled</u> you're
          leaving, it's like they're <u>high</u> on something. . . .

                              GRACE
                    (laughs; to Nurse)
          'Bye, now!

                              JOSIE
                    (to Nurse)
          Never again!
                    (beat)
          See you in six months!
                    (as they pull away)
          Good-bye, Cruella!

INT. CITY RESTAURANT—DAY

Harry approaches maitre d' when he sees TOMMY LASZLO waving
at him from b.g. CAMERA FOLLOWS Harry to Tommy's table, where
he slides in next to him.

                              TOMMY
          You're late, you sonofabitch.

                              HARRY
          Light of my life. How are ya's?

                              TOMMY
          <u>Starving.</u> They got a monkfish today to die for.
          You're going in on a soufflé, I already
          ordered—takes forty minutes.

                              HARRY
          You got a parasite, Tommy?

                              TOMMY
          How goes it on the partner front? Any word yet?

                              HARRY
          Nothing definitive.

                              TOMMY
          It's a done deal.

                                                    (CONTINUED)

                              HARRY
I'm supposed to hear within the week.

                              TOMMY
It'll happen.
                              (serious)
I made a decision: I'm unloading the store.

                              HARRY
You just opened it.

                              TOMMY
Harry: What am I doing selling thousand-dollar
vintage eyeglasses on Melrose for? It's <u>pretentious.</u>

                              HARRY
You're always like this when you start something
new. It was the same with the travel agency, and
the tropical fish.

                              TOMMY
Think that's all it is?

                              HARRY
That's all it is. Guess who I saw today?
                              (beat)
Paige Katz.

                              TOMMY
From school? You're kidding. Where?

                              HARRY
She came into the office.

                              TOMMY
How does she look?

                              HARRY
Unbelievable. She had a kid—he disappeared or
something.

                              TOMMY
A custody thing?

                              HARRY
I don't know—she wouldn't tell me much about
the father.

                              TOMMY
Very film noir.

                              HARRY
That's what I said.

                                        (CONTINUED)

As he talks, Harry notices two Men in Suits enter, scan room. They walk through tables toward Man in Bow Tie who sits with attractive woman, laughing. The woman wears distinctive red spectacles—Sally Jesse Raphael-style.

> HARRY
>
> She is really hot—brought back memories, man. She's sitting there, telling me this terrible tale, and all I could think about was the hair on her arms—and bringing her down by the neck. I'm getting <u>aroused.</u> . . .

> TOMMY
>
> She really got to you, huh? It's a fine line between empathy and animal lust.

Men in Suits approach, seizing Man in Bow Tie. He struggles; the table's upset as luncheoners react. After a beat, Harry impulsively intervenes.

> HARRY
>
> Hey, hold on!

Harry's pushed aside as the other brutally punches the Man in Bow Tie's head, bloodying him. They drag him out. Harry gets on feet and goes to window, where he sees Men in Suits put a hood on their quarry and shove him into a black Range Rover that speeds away. Harry returns to the table. The woman in red spectacles nervously gathers her scattered things; Harry helps, though she seems reluctant to accept aid. While Harry does his thing, she glances up at Tommy, who coldly returns the gaze—do they know each other? The woman hurriedly exits. Harry sits back down.

> TOMMY
>
> That was stupid.

> HARRY
>
> Who were they, Tommy, the police? I never saw that—they really <u>hurt</u> that guy.

The vanquished table is reset; the restaurant quickly returns to normal, as if the event was commonplace. Harry is rattled. WAITER enters.

> WAITER
> (to Tommy)
> Do you need more time?

> TOMMY
>
> Tell me about that monkfish again. Harry, I'm telling you—the sauce is killer.

INT. WYCKOFF HOUSE—DINING ROOM/KITCHEN—DAY

Grace and Josie enter. Coty runs to greet them, hugging Josie.
Tambor and Deirdre appear in b.g.

>   COTY
> Hi, Grammie!

>   JOSIE
> Careful there—your grammie might just unravel.

>   GRACE
> How you feeling, baby?

She feels Coty's forehead; he pulls away, clinging to Josie.

>   COTY
> I'm better!

>   JOSIE
> Were you sick, darling?

>   COTY
> I had a bug.

>   TAMBOR
> He always gets better around three—when
> school's out.

>   COTY
> Shut up, Tambor!

Josie grabs her granddaughter, playfully raising her into air.

>   GRACE
>   (to Coty; stern)
> We do <u>not</u> tell people to shut up in this house.

>   JOSIE
>   (to Deirdre; baby talkish)
> Am I the ultimate grandma? Huh? Huh? And are
> you the ultimate baby girl?

>   GRACE
> Careful, Mom—Tambor, take her.

>   JOSIE
>   (hands Deirdre to Nanny)
> Do you have something to say to me, Buddha-
> girl? Do ya? Do ya?

>   GRACE
>   (to Tambor)
> Are their things packed?

>   NANNY
> All set.

                                        (CONTINUED)

GRACE
(to Josie)
I just don't want him going in the pool, okay?

COTY
I said I'm better!

JOSIE
Your mother says no pool: no pool.

Deirdre and the Nanny exit.

COTY
Grammie, watch me rollerblade!

He exits.

JOSIE
(after him)
In a minute, darling.

GRACE
Use the knee guards, Coty!

JOSIE
How's Deirdre's latest guy?

GRACE
All the experts seem to have a different opinion.

JOSIE
That's why they're experts. Don't make yourself
crazy. She'll talk when she's ready; comes from a
long line of willful women, that's all.

COTY (O.S.)
Grammie!

JOSIE
Are you in trouble, Grace?

GRACE
Trouble?

JOSIE
You and Harry.

GRACE
We're fine. Why do you ask?

JOSIE
Just a feeling.

(CONTINUED)

GRACE
Well, it's a <u>wrong</u> feeling.

JOSIE
He still seeing the shrink?

GRACE
(nods)
He's having nightmares.

EXT. WYCKOFF HOUSE—BACK YARD—DAY

The palms shimmy in the wind. The pool has been drained. Coty rollerblades around on its bottom. Josie emerges from house, watches.

She calls him and he skates over to shallow end.

JOSIE
C'mere, you.

COTY
I had the dream again—last night. The rhinoceros . . .

JOSIE
Tell anyone?
(shakes his head over and over)
Not even your dad?

COTY
Will your butler serve us lunch at the pool?

JOSIE
Yes, monkey-child.

COTY
I want what we ordered last time.

JOSIE
A Monte Cristo.

COTY
With French fries—and the sundaes that come in little silver cups.

JOSIE
Oh, what a demanding monkey-child you are.
(towels his hair)
You're not afraid, are you, darling monkey? If you're afraid of the rhino, the dream goes away. Then you'll be like everybody else. And that's the most terrible thing in the world. . . .

(CONTINUED)

INT. THERAPIST'S OFFICE—DAY

Cool, dark office. Harry sits in a leather chair opposite his therapist, DR. TOBIAS SCHENKL. Schenkl is black, 50s—dignified.

> HARRY
> Grace and I haven't made love in two months.
> That's a record, except for when she had her
> ectopic.

> TOBIAS
> It happens. Couples go through periods. . . .

> HARRY
> You know, I always promised myself a beach
> house; we were supposed to have a beach house
> by now. I couldn't even give Grace the money for
> her store—she had to go to her mother.

> TOBIAS
> Do you think she loves you any less?

> HARRY
> An old lover came to the office this
> morning—awakened something. . . .
> (beat)
> Then, something strange happened, at
> lunch—sorry I'm so unfocussed, Doc. These men
> came into the restaurant and dragged a guy out; it
> looked like one of those dumb Robert Longo
> paintings. Everyone went right back to their meals,
> like it was all staged or something; like it was
> nothing.

> TOBIAS
> You felt . . . vulnerable?

> HARRY
> No. I identified with the men.
> (beat)
> I was rooting for the attackers.

INT. WYCKOFF HOUSE—DINING ROOM—NIGHT

Grace, in Harry's arms, before the fire. They drink wine. Coty and Deirdre are gone—we sense they're able to breathe.

> GRACE
> I really like this.

> HARRY
> Maybe Josie could keep the kids. I'm only talking
> a year or two.

GRACE
She'd <u>love</u> it. Harry . . . have you noticed
anything about Coty?

HARRY
You mean the facial paralysis?

GRACE
He seems . . . distant—he's closer to Mother than
he is to me.

HARRY
That's normal. Boys his age start pulling away.

GRACE
Do they, Dr. Bettelheim? Something about the
look on his face when I touch him—guess I'm just
paranoid.

HARRY
I love that quality.

GRACE
Oh, I forgot to tell you—Deirdre talked.

HARRY
(stunned)
You're kidding.

GRACE
Right before she left with Mother.

HARRY
How could you forget something like that?

GRACE
I don't know why, I just did.

HARRY
For chrissakes, Grace, what'd she say?

GRACE
I went to kiss her. She looked at me and said,
'Everything must go.'

HARRY
Are you sure?

GRACE
It's too freaky to make up, Harry.

HARRY
<u>Everything must go.</u> . . .

(CONTINUED)

> GRACE
> Tell me that you love me, Junie Moon.

> HARRY
> I love you, Junie Moon.

> GRACE
> Mean it?

> HARRY
> I really mean it.

> GRACE
> Show me.

MASTER BEDROOM—CLOSE ON TV SCREEN

A late night Talk-show Host stands at his desk. The VOLUME is LOW; barely audible.

> TALK-SHOW HOST (V.O.)
> A warm welcome for . . . Tabba Schwartzkopf!

Tabba comes from wings to wild applause. She wears a very tight, very short black dress. CAMERA PANS O.S. TO Harry and Grace, making love. We HOLD ON their efforts; after beat, Harry rolls off, frustrated. Stares at ceiling. We hear the dull, tinny laughter of the TELEVISION O.S.

> GRACE
> It's all right, darling.
> (he doesn't respond)
> Darling?

He turns away. Hurt, Grace lays on her side—back to back. After a beat, Harry walks out of room past TV screen. We HOLD ON image of Tabba Schwartzkopf, laughing with forced hilarity at something Host said.

INT. WYCKOFF HOUSE—KITCHEN—NIGHT

Harry goes to refrigerator, opens it. Removes carton of juice. Hears something that makes him pause; a confusion of ROUGH SOUNDS. Slowly, his hand goes to light switch. The overhead fluorescent lights flicker then hold, washing the room in brightness.

CLOSE—JUICE CARTON

hits the floor, explodes.

CLOSE—RHINOCEROS

crammed into the small space. It faces him, impassively. Harry runs.

(CONTINUED)

MASTER BEDROOM

He turns on the light. Grace lays in bed on stomach, sheet over her.

> HARRY
> Grace! Wake up! Wake up—

In stirring her, he moves sheet. He notes detail of coloring on her back. He pulls sheet down to reveal massive tattoo: a palm tree, blurrily blown. Its base disappears at her buttocks. He gently turns her over—revealing "rhino" tattoo, its massive horn bisecting her breasts. Grace's arms conceal her face.

> HARRY
> Oh God . . .

Harry lifts the arms and gasps: It isn't Grace at all—it's the jogger—Senator Tony Kreutzer. Weirdly, the face begins to SQUEAL and tremble, as if an electric current surges through the very lips. The SQUEAL GROWS LOUDER, becomes piercing.

MASTER BEDROOM

Harry awakens with a scream—apparently, all since his impotence was a dream. Grace turns on the nightstand lamp.

> GRACE
> (frightened)
> Oh God! Baby! Harry!

> HARRY
> What's happening to me?

Grace holds him in her arms. Staring impassively into space, she rocks him.

> FADE OUT.

<u>END OF ACT ONE</u>

ACT TWO

FADE IN:

INT. HEALTH CLUB—RACQUETBALL COURT—DAY

Harry and Tommy's fierce game—Harry lets it all out; the impotence, the anger, the confusion. He stumbles; nose bleeds.

JUICE BAR

Harry and Tommy sit with racquets and gym bags, at a table opposite racquetball courts.

> HARRY
> It's these nightmares . . . I keep dreaming of this—rhinoceros.

He laughs.

> TOMMY
> Go on.

> HARRY
> Only it's not like a dream, Tommy, not even close. I walk into a room, and it's there—real as this.

> TOMMY
> I was reading an article—if it's any help. Talked about schizophrenia as an allergy—

> HARRY
> Now I'm schizophrenic?

> TOMMY
> Could be a diet thing.

> HARRY
> (ironic)
> That's probably it. I'll just cut back on cholesterol.

> TOMMY
> The rhino: very sexual. The powder of the horns—a heavy aphrodisiac.

> HARRY
> (re: his impotence)
> That's a hoot.

> TOMMY
> Have you seen a doctor? I mean, what does your shrink say—what's his name?

(CONTINUED)

                              HARRY
Schenkl. He says I'm about to learn important
childhood stuff—I'm having some sort of
breakthrough.

                              TOMMY
Nervous breakthrough.
   (sees something O.S.; urgently whispers)
Harry! Over there—turn slowly. . . . See it?

                              HARRY
                        (turns slowly)
No . . .

                              TOMMY
Beside the StairMaster—

                              HARRY
The girl? What, Tommy?

                              TOMMY
The <u>rhino</u> . . .

                              HARRY
                           (pissy)
I shouldn't of mentioned it.

                              TOMMY
You gotta joke about it, Harry. If you don't joke
about it, you're going to wake up one day and
find yourself at a watering hole, next to a gazelle.

                              HARRY
                          (stands)
See you, Tommy.

                              TOMMY
                  (as they start to walk)
You free tonight?

                              HARRY
What's goin' on?

                              TOMMY
I'm having a few people over. Why don't you
come by—nine o'clock. There's people you
should meet.

                              HARRY
Catch you later.

                              TOMMY
                        (after him)
And bring Grace!

                                          (CONTINUED)

Harry exits. Tommy watches him go, his smile dissolving to cold expressionlessness—their discussion's had an impact. He knows something. . . .

EXT. DARYL F. GATES ELEMENTARY—DAY

Grace hurriedly enters the large brick building.

INT. DARYL F. GATES ELEMENTARY—DAY

Grace enters counseling office—couches and colorful posters. Coty sits glumly on a chair. She sits down, puts arm around him. He stares straight ahead.

> GRACE
> (softly)
> Hi, darling. You okay?

He shrugs. DR. SONDRA WEST, a handsome woman in her early 40s, enters. She wears her long blonde hair in a pontytail.

> WEST
> I'm Dr. West.

> GRACE
> I'm Grace, Coty's mother.

> WEST
> (warmly)
> I gathered that. May we talk a moment?

INT. DR. WEST'S OFFICE—DAY

She closes door, sits at desk—Grace opposite. A "War Is Not Healthy For Children . . ." poster on the wall. Grace is anxious; the friendly doctor tries to soothe her.

> WEST
> We met at open house—you have a little girl . . .

> GRACE
> Yes—Deirdre. Can you tell me what happened?

> WEST
> Coty got into a fight with one of the boys—nothing serious. It's our policy to send kids home when they act out physically. Gives them time to cool off—and think about what they did.

> GRACE
> He's never been in a fight before. Over what?

(CONTINUED)

> WEST
> His class was making family trees—you know,
> tracing history. One of the kids was teasing him.

She hands her a large poster, with a small scraggly line drawn on it.
Coty and Deirdre's name written at bottom, Harry's faintly at top.

> WEST
> What's wrong with this picture?

> GRACE
> He left me off.

> WEST
> Usually, that means a child's angry. Are there
> problems at home?

> GRACE
> No—I mean, it's not the Brady Bunch. . . . He's
> been a little withdrawn. Do you think someone
> molested him?

> WEST
> (smiles)
> I don't want to make this into something it isn't.
> Does he share things with you?

> GRACE
> He used to.

> WEST
> It's a difficult age. Talk to him, Mom. Talk to him,
> and he'll be fine.

> GRACE
> I will. I'll try.

EXT. SCHOOL—DAY

Grace and Coty walk past empty schoolyard to car. Coty is still
withdrawn but seems relieved to be outdoors. Grace is
solicitous—and a little awkward.

> GRACE
> You hit a boy, huh.

> COTY
> He hit me first.

> GRACE
> Did you hurt him?
> (as he shakes his head)
> You mad at me, baby?
> (as he shakes head again)
> You left Mommy off the tree. How come?

(CONTINUED)

> COTY
> It's a stupid class.

> GRACE
> Aren't you interested in where you came from?

> COTY
> I don't care.

> GRACE
> If you ever want to talk to me about
> anything—anything at all—I'm here. I'm your
> mom. Okay?

> COTY
> Okay. Can I go to the movies?

Grace doesn't answer. He jumps into the car; she hesitates a beat before getting in—as if she doesn't know what to make of him.

EXT. DEPARTMENT OF JUSTICE—DAY

Harry enters the smog-stained stone building.

INT. DEPARTMENT OF JUSTICE—MISSING PERSONS BUREAU—DAY

Harry stands at counter clearing his throat, trying to get the attention of a thin-faced BUREAUCRAT who's buried in files.

> HARRY
> I'm investigating a missing child.

> BUREAUCRAT
> Computers are down.

> HARRY
> Any way to look through the stacks?

> BUREAUCRAT
> You an attorney?

> HARRY
> Yes.

> BUREAUCRAT
> (pushing paper)
> Fill this out.

He slides a form to Harry; Harry notes the Bureaucrat has a PALM TATTOO on one hand.

STACKS

The Bureaucrat leads him through room lit by flickering fluorescent tubes—its size as yet unrevealed. It feels claustrophobic; files impinge from all sides.

> BUREAUCRAT
> Name again?

> HARRY
> Harry Wyckoff.

> BUREAUCRAT
> (impatient)
> I meant the missing party.

> HARRY
> It's Peter Katz.

> BUREAUCRAT
> These are the children—K through Z. They only
> go back fifteen years.

Finally, CAMERA PANS the enormous stacks, filled with tens of thousands of files. We PUSH IN ON Harry, shocked at the number.

EXT. STREET—DAY

Harry drives along. There are files on seat beside him that he's taken from the stacks. He slows; there's commotion on sidewalk. Police pin a group of three men and women to the ground, guns to heads. Harry winces at the violent tableau.

> HARRY
> What . . .

As he picks up speed, an unmarked car with uniformed men rushes to scene from opposite direction. Harry begins to sing—out of sight, out of mind.

> HARRY
> 'Never saw the sun shinin' so bright—never saw
> love feelin' so right' . . .

Something catches his attention.

HARRY'S POV

Paige Katz, at the wheel of a sportscar. A woman in scarf sits in the passenger seat. Harry pulls closer: The woman turns for a beat and stares at him, weirdly, the way the jogging Senator did—as if staring through him. The woman appears to be his mother-in-law.

CONTINUED:

> HARRY
> (to self)

Josie?

> (speeds up)

This is crazy.

He tries to catch them, but can't. The valet takes Paige's car; the two women enter hotel. Harry pulls up, follows them in.

INT. HOTEL—DAY

He enters lobby, sees them taking stairs to mezzanine. He's held up for a moment by a bellman who crosses his path with a baggage cart.

BANQUET ROOM

He catches up with Paige as she climbs the stairs—the woman in scarf is gone.

> HARRY

Paige?

> PAIGE

Harry! What are you doing here?

> HARRY

Are you with Josie?

She's nonplussed.

> HARRY

My <u>mother-in-law</u> . . .

> PAIGE
> (laughs)

Your mother-in-law?

> HARRY

She had a scarf—

> PAIGE

Harry, I'm late . . .

> HARRY
> (embarrassed; shifts gears)

Listen . . . I was just at the Justice Department—Missing Persons. You can't believe how many kids have disappeared—

> PAIGE

We'll talk about it later. Come with me, okay?

BANQUET ROOM

(CONTINUED)

They enter. The space is filled with tables of luncheoners; they sit. Onstage, a backdrop of an enormous palm tree—across it, a banner reads: IS IT REAL OR IS IT MIMECOM? On the dais, a SPEAKER addresses the audience.

> SPEAKER
> . . . Now, technology for cheap reality is here—and the Wild Palms Group is in the eye of the postsymbolic storm. Ladies and gentlemen, it is my great honor, through the joint effort of our friends—partners—in Kawasaki and Kansai, to introduce a visionary: tomorrow's realitician and today's bridge between human wetware and high-end telepresence—Senator Tony Kreutzer!

A burst of applause as the Senator takes the stage; Harry has a shock of recognition.

> SENATOR
> Thank you, and welcome. You know, I was in Tokyo just last week—in Japan, they call me Fuji, cause I'm white on top.
> (laughter)
> To paraphrase Aristophanes, I have all the traits of a popular politico: bad breeding, vulgar manner, and a terrific head of hair.

While the audience laughs uproariously, a samurai swordsman enters from the stage left, approaching the Senator. Kreutzer notices him and smiles, as if it's some stunt he's waiting to be let in on. The swordsman unsheaths his weapon and the room grows slightly apprehensive. Harry and Paige watch with interest. The swordsman charges: still half-thinking it's a gag, the audience gasps and nervously laughs at once.

> SENATOR
> Wha—

He raises hands defensively as sword comes down—and passes through him, as if he isn't corporeal. The swordsman slices again and again, to no effect. Suddenly, the samurai figure evaporates, causing another burst of audience emotion. The Senator faces them now, smiling. He speaks very quickly.

> SENATOR
> I'm not here, children: I am a synthetic hologram, talking to you real-time from the penthouse of this hotel. One day very soon, this is what it's gonna look like, right in the living room—you will co-star in weekly sitcoms; you will fight the samurai battles and experience the heartbreak of first love, all between commercials! If you've got a T.V., any old T.V., and an adaptor you get from MimeCom
> (MORE)

> SENATOR (CONT'D)
> for under a thousand dollars—then you've bought
> a ticket. I have seen the future, and it is Channel
> Three!

The audience is on its feet, roaring approval. Harry and Paige join the ovation.

BANQUET ROOM—A WHILE LATER

The luncheon is over. The Senator mingles with the crowd like a popular politician, working his way over to Harry and Paige.

> HARRY
> That's who you work for? The guy who founded
> that religion in the Sixties?

> PAIGE
> Synthiotics. It's helped a lot of people.

> HARRY
> 'New Realism.' Very hip now. Read about it in
> People.

> PAIGE
> Don't be so cynical. You should read some of his
> books.

> HARRY
> I don't dig bad science fiction.

WILLIAM GIBSON approaches from b.g.

> PAIGE
> There's Bill Gibson. . . .

> HARRY
> Oh—"Neuromancer"—

> PAIGE
> Hi, Bill.

> GIBSON
> Hello, Paige.

> PAIGE
> Harry, meet William Gibson. He coined the word
> "cyberspace."
> GIBSON
> And they won't let me forget it.

Gibson exits.

(CONTINUED)

The Senator reaches them. Nearby, at all times, are a cordon of Men
in Suits, watching the crowd. There is an official photographer who
takes the Senator's photo at intervals.

                    SENATOR
                  (kisses her)
          Paige Katz!

                    PAIGE
          Quite a performance, Senator.

                    SENATOR
          Did you really think so?

                    PAIGE
          Very Orson Welles—very Mercury Theatre.

                    SENATOR
          'Invaders From Mars.' We're bringing the whole
          dog and pony show to the FCC next week. Think
          it'll play?

                    PAIGE
          If they like Monopoly. Tony, I want you to meet a
          friend of mine—Harry Wyckoff.

                    SENATOR
          Hello.
                  (to Paige)
          Close friend?

                    PAIGE
          We went to school together.

                    SENATOR
          See the show, Harry?

                    HARRY
          It was mind-boggling.

                    SENATOR
          What do you do, Harry?

                    HARRY
          I'm a lawyer.

                    SENATOR
                  (nodding approval)
          'The armies of the night.'
                  (intimate)
          My father owned a little clothing store in
          downtown L.A., did you know that? Started out a
          tailor. Oh yes—the Jews weren't the only tailors.
          My father was murdered by the Friends.

                                        (CONTINUED)

The Senator's hand is on Harry's shoulder—Harry notices a Palm Tattoo.

> SENATOR
> They broke into his shop and stole his things, they defecated in his shop and they beat this old man, this <u>maker of suits.</u> . . . They didn't kill him; that came months later. He stayed alive long enough to have a fire sale. A fire sale in an inferno, can you imagine it, Harry? I'll never forget the sight of him, death already in the eyes, slumped on a chair beneath a great colorful banner: <u>everything must go.</u>

EXT. LOS ANGELES ZOO—DAY

Uncrowded and overcast. They stroll the meandering walkways between cages and habitats. A light mist falls.

> HARRY
> What the hell was <u>that</u> all about?

> PAIGE
> He's bigger than life, huh.

> HARRY
> (laughs)
> <u>Scary.</u>

> PAIGE
> All he's saying is there's more than one reality—that doesn't make Synthiotoics any different from Buddhism.

> HARRY
> And the Senator just bought Channel Three, right? That's a nice little temple.
> (beat)
> Paige . . . can you tell me about the boy—Peter's—father?

> PAIGE
> Relax, Harry—it isn't you.

> HARRY
> I wasn't implying that. Is there something between you and the Senator?

> PAIGE
> No.

> HARRY
> Was there?

(CONTINUED)

> PAIGE
> Maybe a flirtation, during the early campaign—we
> shared a lot of small planes. It never went beyond
> that.

They pause before the rhino habitat.

> PAIGE
> It takes sixteen months for one of them to make a
> baby. Can you imagine? Of course, you can't. I
> only had Peter for nine. . . .

Suddenly, Harry grabs her; they embrace. He kisses her
softly—making up for all the lost years. He slowly disentangles
himself.

> HARRY
> Paige—I . . . I can't do this. . . .

> PAIGE
> Can't blame a girl for trying.

> HARRY
> It's just that . . . Grace—

She silences him with a finger to his lips.

> PAIGE
> I know. It's okay.

She kisses him gently on the lips.

> PAIGE
> But: As the Buddhists say . . . there's more than
> one reality.

She smiles, exits. Harry watches her a beat before following.

> FADE OUT.

END OF ACT TWO

<u>ACT THREE</u>

FADE IN:

INT. WYCKOFF HOUSE—DEIRDRE'S ROOM—NIGHT

Harry's dressed to go out. He sits on daughter's bed; she's under the covers. He caresses her little head—determined to gently get to the bottom of her mysterious utterance.

> HARRY
> Everything must go. <u>Everything must go.</u> Did you really say that, Little Buddha? Huh?

> GRACE (O.S.)
> Harry, come on! We'll be late—

He kisses her; DEIRDRE GIGGLES as he nuzzles.

> HARRY
> Nightie-night, sleep-monster.

Tambor stands in doorway. Harry exits.

> HARRY
> (to nanny)
> Be home by midnight.

INT. CORVETTE—NIGHT

Harry and Grace, as they wind their way to Tommy's party.

> HARRY
> Did you have your talk with Coty?

> GRACE
> More like a monologue—mine.

> HARRY
> Everyone reads too much into it—the kid's just bored; way ahead of his class.

> GRACE
> I guess.

> HARRY
> I thought I saw your mother today.

> GRACE
> She's in Palm Springs.

> HARRY
> I know. But I thought I saw her in this car. I even followed it.

(CONTINUED)

GRACE
Where'd it go?

HARRY
Over a cliff. Just kidding.

GRACE
Did she have a big horn?

Harry doesn't laugh.

GRACE
Sorry. Is it any better?

HARRY
Is what?

GRACE
You know. The problem.

HARRY
(amusing)
You have to be a little more specific, honey. I
mean, we got a lot goin' on here: nightmares,
impotence, trouble with the kids—

They laugh together.

INT. TOMMY'S HOUSE—LIVING ROOM—NIGHT

Harry and Grace enter crowded house—they're a little party-shy; out
of their element. Artist and bohemian types. Tabba is there with her
boyfriend, TULLY WOIWODE, the famous artist. He's in his forties,
sly, seductive and drunk. She sees Grace.

TABBA
Hey, there!

GRACE
Hi! What are <u>you</u> doing here?

TABBA
Using the bathroom, what else. I forgot your—

GRACE
Grace.

TABBA
You were <u>hilarious</u>—I was gonna call you.

GRACE
This is my husband, Harry Wyckoff.

TABBA
Your wife is <u>fantastic.</u>

(CONTINUED)

                        WOIWODE
"Mr. Wyckoff Goes to Washington." Wasn't that a
movie?

                        TABBA
Maybe in your mind, it was. This is my consort,
Tully Woiwode.

                        HARRY
I'm a big fan. I was lobbying to get one of your
paintings into the atrium—the 'Watchers, What of
the Night?' triptych.

                        WOIWODE
                        (grandly)
'The morning cometh, and also the night: The dog
is turned to his own vomit again . . .'

                        TABBA
That's disgusting!

                        TOMMY
                        (enters; also drunk)
Babylon has fallen!

                        GRACE
Tommy, we didn't know you knew these guys.

                        TOMMY
Forever.

                        GRACE
                        (to Tabba)
He's been hoarding you.

                        HARRY
Is there food?

                        TOMMY
Baby, is there ever! But first, there's booze—gotta
clean that palate.

                        WOIWODE
I got a palate so clean, I could eat off it.

                        TABBA
Somebody take him. He needs food.

                        WOIWODE
                        (exiting, with Tommy and Grace; sings)
'I'm just wild about Harry.' . . .

                        HARRY
Happy guy.

                                        (CONTINUED)

                                TABBA
                                (smiles)
          Little <u>too</u> happy.

                                HARRY
          I saw that thing you did with Jimmy
          Wolcott—what was it?

                                TABBA
          'All Fall Down.'

                                HARRY
          You were terrific. You know, my son acts.
                                (as she nods, bored)
          Working on anything?

                                TABBA
          Something for Channel Three.

"UPTIGHT, OUTTA SIGHT" LOUDLY ON SPEAKERS. People start
dancing; Grace pulls Tabba by the arm.

                                Grace
          Come on!

They dance as Tommy enters; CAMERA TRACKS WITH Harry and
Tommy as they move off.

                                TOMMY
          What do you think of Tully Woiwode?

                                HARRY
          Does he paint anymore?

                                TOMMY
          He's a <u>factory</u>—the Schnabel of the West Coast.
          Even does <u>restaurant menus.</u> Know what they call
          him? The Merchant of Venice!

The party's raucous now. Across crowded room, Harry sees someone
familiar—the woman in red spectacles who he saw at the City.

                                HARRY
          Tommy, who is that? In the red glasses?

                                TOMMY
          Mazie Woiwode . . .

                                HARRY
          She's the one from the restaurant. You mean, you
          <u>know</u> her?

                                VOICE (O.S.)
          Tommy, get your ass over here!

                                                    (CONTINUED)

Tommy exits as we TRACK WITH Harry until he reaches WOMAN,
AD LIBS hello.

> HARRY
> I was at City when those guys grabbed your
> friend. What happened to him?

> WOMAN (MAZIE)
> (polite)
> You're mixing me up with someone.

> HARRY
> I just wanted to know if he was okay.

> MAZIE
> (cold)
> It's a <u>mistake.</u>

She abruptly tries to leave, but blunders into a drunken Woiwode.
STEVIE WONDER'S "Ma Cherie Amour" begins; Woiwode sings it to
Woman.

> WOIWODE
> '<u>Ma cherie amour</u>—' Wyckoff: Did you meet my
> sister?

Harry and Mazie AD LIB awkward hellos.

> WOIWODE
> Too bad you're married. We're trying to find
> Mazie a suitable candidate for breeding.

INT. BAUM, WEISS, AND LATIMER—DAY

Harry enters conference room. The senior partners—TOM LATIMER,
and SEVERIN WEISS—greet him. Harry senses he's in for something
unpleasant.

> WEISS
> Hello, Harry.

> HARRY
> Severin.

> WEISS
> Joe couldn't make it—he's still fly fishing in some
> top-secret location.

> HARRY
> As long as he brings back a fish story.

> WEISS
> That he will. Joe Baum could bring back a fish
> story from the Gobi.

(CONTINUED)

                         LATIMER
A woman came to see you—Paige Katz.

                          HARRY
An old friend.

                         LATIMER
Did you know that Ms. Katz is a consultant for the
Wild Palms Group?

                          HARRY
She may have mentioned it.

                          WEISS
You also know that we're preparing a suit against
MimeCom on behalf of the Deake Newhouse
Company.

                          HARRY
I haven't been involved in that, but I heard
something about it.

                         LATIMER
It seems someone from Newhouse found out Ms.
Katz was visiting our offices.

                          HARRY
She came to me because of a personal problem.

                          WEISS
                         (smiles)
No one's accusing you—or your friend—of being
a mole, Harry.

                          HARRY
That's comforting.

                          WEISS
Deake Newhouse is concerned enough to have
threatened to go elsewhere.

                         LATIMER
This account means a lot to us, as you well know.

                          WEISS
It would be impolitic for us to give you a full
partnership just now. The timing isn't good.

                          HARRY
This is absurd. Paige Katz is in trouble. Her son
disappeared—

                          WEISS
When was the last time you saw her?

                                    HARRY
                    Awhile. Fifteen years, maybe.

                                    LATIMER
                    A woman you haven't seen for fifteen years drops
                    by to ask a patent attorney to help her find her
                    son. How does it sound, Harry?

                                    HARRY
                    I really don't care, Severin. Why am I starting to
                    feel like I'm in a courtroom?

                                    WEISS
                    There's no need . . .

                                    HARRY
                    I want that partnership, Severin. You <u>owe</u> me—

                                    WEISS
                    We're going to make Morty Winakur a limited
                    partner; when things cool down with Stratton,
                    we'll take you aboard—with open arms.

                                    HARRY
                                   (realizing)
                    Morty Winakur?

                                    WEISS
                    Let things settle, Harry.

                                    HARRY
                                   (stands)
                    Yeah, I will. But they can settle without me.

                                    LATIMER
                    You're being foolish.

                                    HARRY
                    See yas.

He exits.

OUTSIDE OFFICES

Harry practically runs into Morty Winakur.

                                    MORTY
                    You okay?

                                    HARRY
                    <u>Slimy little prick.</u>

He pushes past him. Paula watches scene from b.g. as Winakur
manages to look offended.

                                                    (CONTINUED)

INT./EXT. OPTIMAL VIEW—DAY

Harry talks to Tommy as they walk outside Tommy's store, onto Melrose. They sit down on bus bench.

> HARRY
>
> Come on, Tommy—it's a little <u>Byzantine,</u> don't you think? If Paige wanted someone to think we were in collusion, why the rigmarole about her kid?

> TOMMY
> (shrugs)
>
> It's an eat-what-you-shoot world, Harry. Have you told Grace yet—I mean, about work?

> HARRY
> (shakes head)
>
> It just happened. I was counting on that partnership—how the hell am I going to get my beach house?

> TOMMY
>
> What are you going to do?

> HARRY
>
> I'm calling time-out. I didn't realize how tired I was—or how bored.

> TOMMY
> (mock-serious)
>
> I can always use another salesman. Seriously: You really gonna quit?

> HARRY
> (laughs)
>
> I'm really gonna quit.

INT. WYCKOFF HOUSE—LIVING/DINING ROOM—DAY

Grace and Coty enter. Coty plunks himself in front of TV. Harry, in apron, enters from kitchen with Deirdre in arms.

> GRACE
>
> Hi, darling. Hmmm . . . whatcha cookin' in there?

> HARRY
>
> Pork chops, baby—King of Pork Chop Hill.

> GRACE
> (to Coty)
>
> Tell Daddy what happened. Come on, tell him.

Coty ignores her.

(CONTINUED)

                                    GRACE
Mister Cool Customer.

                                    HARRY
Kill someone at school?

                                    GRACE
Coty . . .

                                    COTY
I'm gonna be on television.

                                    GRACE
Tabba's new show, 'Church Windows.'

                                    HARRY
How'd that happen?

                                    GRACE
We had lunch. She said they were looking for a
twelve-year-old kid for her show. I told her about
Coty and she said, bring him in.

                                    COTY
                              (re: TV show)
Quiet!

He turns UP VOLUME.

                                    HARRY
Does he even want to do this, Grace?

                                    GRACE
                              (deadpan)
Oh, it's torture for him. Of course, he wants to!

The DOORBELL RINGS.

                                    COTY
I'll get it!

Coty runs for it.

                                    HARRY
You didn't comment on the apron.

                                    GRACE
                              (looks it over)
It's almost erotic.

                                    HARRY
I'm gonna play house-husband for awhile.

                                    GRACE
Call me Yoko. . . .

                                                      (CONTINUED)

                                    HARRY
                    I quit the firm today.

Grace reacts.

                                    COTY
                                  (entering)
                    It's a lady.

We TRACK WITH Harry as he walks to door: Paige Katz. He's a little
unsettled.

                                    PAIGE
                    Hello, Harry.

                                    HARRY
                    What are you doing here?

Grace ENTERS FRAME, smiling inquisitively, still thrown by Harry's
news.

                                    HARRY
                                  (awkward)
                    Grace, this is Paige Katz, an old friend—and a
                    client.

                                    GRACE
                    Hi.

                                    PAIGE
                    Sorry to burst in on you like this.

                                    HARRY
                    We were just sitting down to an early supper—

                                    GRACE
                    That's all right, Harry.

                                    PAIGE
                    It won't take but a minute. Can we talk outside?

Harry points the way, throws Grace a baffled shrug as he follows the
visitor, removing apron. We HOLD ON Grace.

EXT. WYCKOFF HOUSE—BACK YARD—DAY

They walk along the empty pool; a soft wind blows leaves into it.

                                    HARRY
                    What are you doing here?

                                    PAIGE
                    I had to see you. Talk to you.

                                                        (CONTINUED)

> HARRY
> Paige, you should probably find someone else to
> follow up on your son. I—I just don't think this is
> such a great idea . . .

Some of the following dialogue will be in V.O. as we ANGLE ON
Grace, watching from behind sliding glass door, assessing her
husband's involvement with this seductive woman, troubled. Then
she turns her back, exiting.

> PAIGE
> I called your office—they said you'd taken leave.
> A friend of mine had a dream about you. He
> wants you to come and see him, in Rancho
> Mirage.

> HARRY
> The Senator?

> PAIGE
> He wanted me to give you this.

She hands him a paper. Harry opens it—a detailed drawing of a
rhino's head.

> FADE OUT.

END OF ACT THREE

ACT FOUR

FADE IN:

EXT. DESERT HIGHWAY/RANGE ROVER—DAY

A Range Rover passes hills of energy windmills on the way to its
destination. Men in Suits in front seat; Harry in back, looking out.

EXT. WILD PALMS—DAY

A vast, walled compound in Rancho Mirage. The Range Rover is
waved through a massive gate, flanked by armed men. The car parks
and Harry is greeted by more Men in Suits, ushered into house.

EXT. GOLF COURSE—DAY

The estate's private course. Harry's pointed in direction of the
Senator, putting on the green. Harry approaches, then stands still as
the ball goes toward the hole, drops in. A caddy retrieves it then runs
to golf cart and waits. Harry moves closer. Throughout scene, a row
of palms is buffeted by breezes.

                    SENATOR
          Enjoy the desert, Harry?

                    HARRY
          Very much.

                    SENATOR
          The winds are constant in this spot—that's why
          we call it Wild Palms. It's a sanctuary to me.

He walks; Harry follows.

                    HARRY
          When I was a boy, I ran away from home. Took a
          bus to Palm Springs.

                    SENATOR
                    (laughs)
          I like that—running away to the desert! 'The wind
          is old and still at play/while I must hurry upon my
          way/For I am running to Paradise.'

                    HARRY
          That's Yeats.

                    SENATOR
          You're gonna make me fall in love with you,
          Harry.
                    (beat)
          We live in a desert—that's the world. We
                    (MORE)

                                        (CONTINUED)

                         SENATOR (CONT'D)
inherited it; no sense complaining. Some of us
want to see it become a garden again. The mass
graves of children . . .

                         HARRY
What?

                         SENATOR
          (swings at ball on tee; watches it arc)
Not far from here, they found it: a lost city of
children's imaginings.

                         HARRY
That drawing Paige gave me. I had some
nightmares—

                         SENATOR
          (they begin to walk)
You know what the rhino is, Harry? It's all that's
left of the unicorn. A magnificent atavism—the
remnant of ecstatic myth. Rough and nearly blind;
utterly exquisite.
          (laughs)
You think I'm a tweaked old bastard, don't you?

                         HARRY
Maybe.

                         SENATOR
How would you like to work for me?

                         HARRY
Doing what?

                         SENATOR
          (caddy places ball on tee)
We'd have to find something. Household chores,
maybe? Can always use another masseur. How
about head of business affairs at Channel Three, at
five times your old salary?

He tees off.

                         HARRY
          (dodges dirt clump)
Are you kidding?

                         SENATOR
Absolutely not.

                         HARRY
Why me?

                                              (CONTINUED)

SENATOR
Two reasons: Because I dreamt about Harry
Wyckoff and the unicorn—and because when you
were just a boy, you ran away . . . to the desert.

INT. WYCKOFF HOUSE—LIVING ROOM—DAY

Grace sits on the floor in the darkened room. She's been drinking;
spread out before her is a massive jigsaw puzzle.

GRACE
How was it?

HARRY
Pretty amazing. He's got a house the size of a
country club.

GRACE
(ironic)
Are you a spokesman for Synthiotics now?

HARRY
Not quite. But he asked me to work for him.

GRACE
(stands; goes to wetbar)
Gonna do it?

HARRY
It's a lot of money. I just have to figure out what
I'm getting myself into.

GRACE
Drink?
(after a beat)
Why didn't you tell me about her?

HARRY
Paige? I don't know—it was all a long time ago.
Maybe I should have.

GRACE
Were you still seeing her? When we first met?
(beat)
Don't lie to me, Harry.

HARRY
No. It was over a few months before.

GRACE
Is it over now?

HARRY
Yes.

> GRACE
> Got you on the rebound, huh.

> HARRY
> You're the best thing that ever happened to me,
> Grace.

> GRACE
> I used to think so.
> (stands)
> I have a headache. I'm gonna take a nap.

> HARRY
> I love you.

> GRACE
> (reaches stairs; without looking back)
> Love you, too. It's a world filled with giant
> lovebugs.

He watches her go—he's feeling guilty about the kiss at the zoo.
Stranded.

HALLWAY—STAIRS—SAME TIME

Darkness. Coty has been listening to his parents. He hears Grace
coming, then walks down hall.

DEIRDRE'S ROOM—SAME TIME

Coty enters. Deirdre stands in front of window, looking out. He joins
her; she doesn't acknowledge him. He looks out at what she's staring
at—the wild palms, buffeted by the wind.

EXT. SUNSPOT—NIGHT

Harry and Tommy (Tommy's car) pull off highway and stop in front
of a ruined nightclub, gutted by fire: "ON THE ROX KOMEDY
KLUB." We can hear WAVES CRASHING O.S.

> HARRY
> What are we doing here?

> TOMMY
> You always wanted a beach house, didn't you?
> Well, I found you one.

> HARRY
> I thought we were having dinner. I'm <u>starving.</u>

> TOMMY
> There's something inside I want to show you . . .

They exit car toward club. Tommy starts to peel back the chain-link
fence that surrounds it.

(CONTINUED)

> TOMMY
> You've been looking into missing kids, right?

> HARRY
> Yeah.

> TOMMY
> Remember all those kidnappings during the Nineties? That was a secret recruitment program for the Fathers. . . .

> HARRY
> (cynical)
> The 'Fathers'? What are we talking about, satanists?

> TOMMY
> Too 'political' for you, Harry?

> HARRY
> I'm listening.

They enter the Sunspot.

INT. SUNSPOT—NIGHT

Harry follows Tommy through the darkness.

> TOMMY
> Poly Sci 101: two groups, okay? Sworn political enemies—one's called the Fathers, the other's called the Friends. The Friends were a watchdog group, Bill of Rights freaks.

> HARRY
> Why are you telling me this?

> TOMMY
> (light)
> Because you've been in a bubble for the last ten years and I want you to stop being a moron.

> CHICKIE (O.S.)
> That you, Tommy?

> TOMMY
> Hey, Chickie! I brought a friend.

They reach an enclosed area within the ruins. Bruch's <u>Kol Nidre</u> ON RADIO. Damp and dark. Then, a tiny light CLICKS ON, illuminating wheelchair-bound CHICKIE LEVITT. No one else is there. Levitt wears reflective silver wraparound shades.

> CHICKIE
> Nice to see you—make yourselves at home.

(CONTINUED)

                            TOMMY
          This is Harry Wyckoff.

                            CHICKIE
          We'll use the ballroom. Why don't you pick out
          eyeglasses for you and your friend?

Chickie points again to an old table with a dozen or so pair of
beautiful spectacles, antique monocles, etc. Harry is baffled, but
Tommy nods at him to follow his lead.

                            TOMMY
          Beautiful. I should sell these back at the store,
          huh, Harry.

Tommy takes two pairs, hands one to Harry. Harry and Tommy put
on glasses; Harry's head jiggles at the invisible onslaught.

                            CHICKIE
                         (to Harry)
          You might be a little nauseous at first—

INT. BALLROOM—SAME TIME

The rest of scene is played within cavernous seventeenth century
ballroom. Harry and Tommy wear brocaded satin and powdered
wigs. Chickie's tall, handsome, and walks unaided—nothing like his
crippled counterpart.

                            CHICKIE
          How's that? Better?

                            HARRY
          What's happening?

                            TOMMY
          This is all computer-generated. We're in
          cyberspace—they call it the Web. Just go with it.

                            HARRY
                         (awed and confused)
          Is it real?

                            CHICKIE
          Or is it MimeCom!

A COMMOTION O.S.—Twenty Soldiers and horses enter frame.
Chickie ignores them, continuing as soldiers amble FROM FRAME.

                            CHICKIE
          It's been twenty years since they broke my back
          and left me for dead. I had to lay under my
          mother's body, very still. Tell you why: After they
          killed her, they sat at the table and had dinner; ate
                         (MORE)

                                                    (CONTINUED)

> CHICKIE (CONT'D)
> the food she'd cooked just hours before. Even
> today, I can feel the weight of her . . .

> HARRY
> You mentioned MimeCom. Do you know the
> Senator?

> CHICKIE
> Our Father, Who art in Heaven, hollow be Thy
> name! The Senator wants a 'map to the
> stars'—don't we all! You know, this burnt out
> nightclub of a world doesn't thrill me in the least
> anymore; soon, I'll fade into the algorithm, won't
> I, Thomas?

He laughs wickedly. TERRA, a slender black ballerina, walks toward
them from far end of ballroom.

> CHICKIE
> Terra! This is Terra—she comes to us all the way
> from Kyoto . . .

> TOMMY
> (to Harry)
> She's plugged into a computer, just like we
> are—only she's in Japan. Both parties are able to
> meet in the Web.

> CHICKIE
> (to Tommy)
> Try and be a little more poetic.

> TERRA
> (a weird, electronic basso)
> Do you want me to come back, Chickie?

> CHICKIE
> Stay—they're just leaving.
> (to Harry and Tommy)
> I call her 'Terra Infirma'—bad joke.
> (to Terra)
> Set your glasses down anywhere, boys. And
> thanks so much for dropping by. Nice to meet
> you, Harry. 'Bye now.

Chickie takes Terra in his arms. Tommy indicates it's time for them to
go, but Harry ignores him, transfixed. Finally, Tommy yanks Harry's
glasses from his head.

INT. SUNSPOT—SAME TIME

The bracing loneliness of old reality. They leave Chickie Levitt in his
wheelchair, holding nothingness.

(CONTINUED)

EXT. SUNSPOT—NIGHT

Tommy and Harry emerge into the cold, windblown night.

>   HARRY
> Too weird! The Web . . . so real! I mean, I've
> played around with virtual reality toys but this!

>   TOMMY
> The Senator wanted Chickie to work for him. See,
> Chickie's the Einstein of the New World—the
> Senator's more like P.T. Barnum. He wants to
> bring that ballroom in there over the phone lines,
> right into the living rooms of America . . .

>   HARRY
> Whoah . . .

>   TOMMY
> That's what Church Windows is all about.

>   HARRY
> That stuff about his mother being murdered . . .

>   TOMMY
> Chickie's parents provided asylum for stolen
> children.

>   HARRY
> How does Chickie survive?

>   TOMMY
> The Friends—the ones who aren't in jail.
> Woiwode and his sister . . .

>   HARRY
> Why didn't you ever tell me, show me this before?

>   TOMMY
> Wasn't a reason.

Harry looks back toward the nightclub in disbelief.

>   HARRY
>   (ecstatic)
> That ballroom! Those horses! I'm telling you,
> Tommy, I'm blown!

INT./EXT. VENICE STUDIO—NIGHT

Tully walks his sister out of the spacious studio, whose walls are
filled with giant expressionistic paintings.

>   MAZIE
> Incredible movie. How old's Jack Nicholson now?

                    WOIWODE
Gotta be close to seventy.

                    MAZIE
That movie really <u>depressed</u> me.

                    WOIWODE
The Indian got away, didn't he?

                    MAZIE
                    (ironic)
Oh, terrific.

                    WOIWODE
Want to get dinner somewhere?

They reach her car.

                    MAZIE
Are you kidding? I o.d.'d on that popcorn of
yours. Think I'll just go home. Where's Tommy?

                    WOIWODE
Out with Harry Wyckoff.

                    MAZIE
                    (teasing)
Jealous?

                    WOIWODE
Tearing my hair out. You know, I really like these
film festival nights of ours.

                    MAZIE
Brothers and sisters share the sweetest mysteries.

                    WOIWODE
Mystery loves company.

                    MAZIE
                    (laughs; kisses him)
Good night.

INT. WILD PALMS—NIGHT

The Senator lays on a table, nude under smallish towel. Lights are
low. Josie's rubbing him down. A wall of televisions tuned to
different channels flickers in b.g. Throughout scene, the Senator is
amused by his sister's flare for vitriol.

                    SENATOR
I want Chickie Levitt brought in—and I want
Woiwode to do it.

                                        (CONTINUED)

                                 JOSIE
            A jewel in the saddle of an ass.

                              SENATOR
            What is it between you and Woiwode? You're
            worse than a Punch-and-Judy show.

                                 JOSIE
            At least we know who Judy is.
                                (beat)
            He betrays you with every breath.

                              SENATOR
            He is a fair painter.

                                 JOSIE
            He's a whore—and you're his biggest john.
            Someone should set him on fire.

                              SENATOR
                                (laughs)
            You're too hard on him. He saved my life.

                                 JOSIE
            And he'll take it away.

                              SENATOR
            I would have drowned . . .

                                 JOSIE
            Don't talk to me about that fateful day in Catalina.
            He almost drowned you just so he could pluck
            you out of the water and get a medal—he wanted
            you forever in his debt. Woiwode knows how soft
            you are.

                              SENATOR
            How soft am I?

                                 JOSIE
            You got the skin of a kid, know that?

EXT. MULHOLLAND—NIGHT

Mazie drives, listening to SUPREMES. She notices bright light in
rearview. It comes up behind her and slams into her bumper; a
Range Rover. The Rover runs her off road. She gets out, clambers
downhill. Men in Suits exit Rover, chasing after her. We HOLD ON
Rover as we hear COMMOTION O.S. We hear her terrible
SCREAMS—she's been seized. The SCREAMS CONTINUE as:

                                                    (CONTINUED)

A figure in black exits Rover, standing on ridge like an empress:
Paige Katz.

FADE OUT.

<u>END OF ACT FOUR</u>

ACT FIVE

FADE IN:

INT. WYCKOFF HOUSE—BEDROOM—DAY

Grace lays in bed in b.g. Harry adjusts tie in mirror, sings:

> HARRY
> 'One child grows up to be . . . someone who just
> loves to learn'—

> GRACE
> Please don't sing, Harry.

> HARRY
> 'Other child grows up to be' . . .

> GRACE
> Harry, come on—

> HARRY
> You don't like my voice?

> GRACE
> I have a headache.

> HARRY
> You mean 'hangover.'

Grace makes a face. He leans over her, singing quietly in her ear, almost a whisper; she kind of likes it.

> HARRY
> 'It's a family affair'—

> GRACE
> Aren't we excited. Nervous?

> HARRY
> Who, me?

> GRACE
> First day of school and all.

> HARRY
> No way.

> GRACE
> Can you check on Coty? He's got a read-through
> at the studio—

(CONTINUED)

                              HARRY
Going into the store today?
                    (as she shakes her head)
I don't think you've been out of this room for <u>five</u>
<u>days.</u>

                              GRACE
I told you. I'm not feeling well.

                              HARRY
That's probably because you're drinking during
the day and on the balcony at night, watching the
damn palms.
                    (beat)
You should talk to my shrink.

                              GRACE
I don't <u>want</u> to talk to your shrink.

                              HARRY
Talk to <u>somebody</u>. I'm outta here.

                              GRACE
Okay, Mr. Head of Business Affairs.

                              HARRY
                    (kisses her)
Try to leave the house today, okay? Take a drive
or something.

                              GRACE
                    (contrite)
Love me?

                              HARRY
                    (sings)
'<u>I love you, baby, and if it's quite all right</u>'—

She swats him out of the room.

EXT. RESIDENTIAL STREETS—MORNING

Harry drives the Corvette, listening to RADIO; feeling good. He
passes a kid on street, around Coty's age. Beside the boy is a sign:
MAPS TO STARS' HOMES. He then backs the car up; the MAPS TO
STARS BOY approaches, proffering map.

                    MAPS TO STARS BOY
Maps to the stars?

He wears a V-neck shirt; Harry notices markings on his chest. The
Boy pulls up shirt, revealing Starry Tattoos. Harry is repelled, fearful
and curious—all at once.

                                            (CONTINUED)

> HARRY
>
> Who . . . did that to you?

> MAPS TO STARS BOY
> (affable)
>
> Church of the Fathers.
> (offers map)
>
> Buy a map?

Spooked, Harry speeds away, BURNING RUBBER.

EXT. WYCKOFF HOUSE—MORNING

Grace stands in robe at front door, waving at her son as station wagon with Channel Three on its door pulls away.

STATION WAGON

Coty watches her coldly, then turns away.

INT. WYCKOFF HOUSE—BEDROOM—MORNING

Grace goes to bottom drawer of dresser, pulls out old manila envelope. She takes the packet back to bed, opens it. She looks at various photos, some black and white, some color. They are pictures of her as a little girl—dressed in a kimono—with a younger Josie, and a man we do not recognize. The man is her father. END ON photo of Grace, around six years old, and father.

EXT. VENICE HOME/STUDIO—DAY

The sunlit art and living space of Tully Woiwode. Suddenly, a BELLOWING SCREAM, as of a wounded animal. Woiwode staggers into courtyard. After a beat, Tommy enters.

> TOMMY
> (rushing to him)
>
> What is it!

> WOIWODE
> (sotto voce)
>
> That _vile cervix_!

Eyes closed, Woiwode extends arm then opens hand to reveal pair of broken red glasses—Mazie's. The lenses have black Xs drawn on them, as if by a felt marker.

> TOMMY
>
> Mazie . . .
> (as Woiwode nods)
>
> What does it mean?

> WOIWODE
>
> _Josie_ did this. . . . Gonna pop that monster!

                                                                (CONTINUED)

TOMMY
Don't make it personal, Tully. The house'll fall
down—

WOIWODE
(picks up glasses)
I'll consider this delivery a kiss. I'm going to show
Josie just how much damage can be done with a
mouth like mine.
(screams)
Hold me, Tommy!
(breaks down)
Hold me!

EXT. CHANNEL THREE—EXECUTIVE OFFICES/STUDIOS—DAY

WPN and its logo grace the high, white-walled facade. Harry pulls
into parking space, already marked: H. WYCKOFF. GAVIN
WHITEHOPE bounds toward him. Whitehope's overweight, but
moves with surprising alacrity. He pumps Harry's hand. In following
scenes, Harry's alternately eager, awkward and amused.

GAVIN
Gavin Whitehope, Public Relations. I'm your
Virgil for today.

HARRY
How are you—

GAVIN
I'm gonna give you the Grand Tour. Been a little
stormy this morning: We're having nuisances with
the Windows copyright, you'll be filled in by
legal—it's transient and ephemeral. Totally
resolvable.

INT. CHANNEL THREE—EXECUTIVE OFFICES/STUDIOS—DAY

His fast-talking guide hustles Harry through busy halls, walls lined
with blow-ups of actors from various hit series. Whitehope flits from
one topic to another.

GAVIN
You hungry?

HARRY
I had breakfast.

GAVIN
You like pasta?

HARRY
Sure . . .

A bald EXEC ENTERS FRAME; late twenties.

(CONTINUED)

> GAVIN
> Phil Bortzman—Harry Wyckoff, new head of
> business affairs.

> HARRY
> Hi, Phil.

> EXEC
> A pleasure!

> GAVIN
> (moving on)
> Phil's daytime. Wife just left him—for his <u>father.</u>

> HARRY
> You're kidding!

Gavin grimly shakes his head. As they EXIT FRAME, CAMERA STAYS
ON photo blow-up: the glamorous Tabba Schwartzkopf.

INT. CITY RESTAURANT—DAY

Lunch with Gavin and Harry. The omnivorous Whitehope wolfs his
food as he casually interrogates his new associate.

> GAVIN
> How long you been married?

> HARRY
> Thirteen years, last month.

> GAVIN
> Can't believe how much I hated that salad. Little
> bits of nectarine in there. Nectarine! Where'd you
> meet?

> HARRY
> College—U.C.L.A.

> GAVIN
> (gulps at wine)
> Oily clumps of . . . <u>gouda</u>—like tiny little men's
> heads. Kids?

> HARRY
> Boy and a girl.

> GAVIN
> I got four—oldest is a cop.

> HARRY
> What'd you do before Channel Three?

(CONTINUED)

> GAVIN
> (holds up pasta on fork)
> Smell the clam sauce—like the sweat of a saint!
> Didn't do so well during the Depression—hand
> me one of those—what is that, pumpernickel?
> (as Harry hands him basket)
> Had some crappy years—like everyone. Got into
> some trouble. Robbed a bank.

> HARRY
> A <u>bank</u>? This was when?

> GAVIN
> Six, seven years ago. You remember how bad it
> got.

> HARRY
> They catch you?

> GAVIN
> Oh yeah. Went to prison.

> HARRY
> Jesus, Gavin!

> GAVIN
> Jail gave me time to think—I know it's a cliché. In
> my worst moment, I got handed a book on
> Synthiotics.

> HARRY
> <u>On the Way to the Garden.</u>

> GAVIN
> You got it. The world's a smoke-filled room,
> Harry. We die in the aisles, looking for the exit.
> The Senator shows the way.

INT. WYCKOFF HOUSE—ENTRANCE/DEN—NIGHT

Harry and his briefcase enter the dark house; home from work. He
sees the flicker of a TV coming from the den. Walks to den; Coty and
Deirdre are planted in front of TV, watching cartoons.

> HARRY
> Hey, killer. Where's your mom?

> COTY
> (eyes on set)
> She's out back.

Harry watches TV commercial.

CLOSE ON GRAPHICS

(CONTINUED)

> They Said the Revolution Wouldn't
> Be Televised.

Dissolve.

> They Were Wrong.

Dissolve.

> CHURCH WINDOWS

Dissolve.

> Coming This Fall.

The Channel Three/WPN logo is supered. Harry exits.

EXT. WYCKOFF HOUSE—POOL—NIGHT

Grace lays on chaise lounge, sips from ice-filled glass. The ever-present wind shoving the trees around. Harry sits at the end, rubs her feet.

> HARRY
> How you doin'?

> GRACE
> (re: foot rub)
> Hmmm—that's nice. It's hot in the house.

> HARRY
> The wind—beautiful.

> GRACE
> I'm going away this weekend. To the desert.

> HARRY
> What's in the desert?

> GRACE
> A friend—someone who knew my stepdad. At the prison hospital in Indian Wells.

> HARRY
> The Resort?
> (as she nods)
> What's he there for?

> GRACE
> It's political.

> HARRY
> Political?

(CONTINUED)

>   GRACE
> I never told you about him. He was an old friend
> of the family—from Kyoto. He founded a
> group . . .
>
>   HARRY
>   (jokey)
> You mean, like a band?
>
>   GRACE
> They're called the Friends.

EXT. WILD PALMS—LAWN—NIGHT

The Senator, Paige and Josie having supper in the formal dining
room. A white-gloved butler serves. The Senator savors his wine,
then:

>   SENATOR
> How is Chickie Levitt?
>
>   PAIGE
> Weak.
>
>   SENATOR
> Has he talked?
>
>   JOSIE
> He will.
>
>   SENATOR
>   (sarcastic)
> You know, you really inspire confidence. Has he
> mentioned the GO chip? You answer me now,
> Josie!
>
>   JOSIE
> Don't you snipe at me! It's only been a few
> weeks—
>
>   SENATOR
>   (shouting)
> We are the cardinals of this cathedral and this
> broken boy is to us as stained glass! He _is_ the
> friggin' church windows—<u>no</u> escape without him!
>
>   PAIGE
> I think he'll talk—to a man. Someone around the
> age his father was, before he was taken. What
> about Chap Starfall?
>
>   SENATOR
> Haven't heard that name in a thousand years.

(CONTINUED)

>   PAIGE
> I talked to him a few months ago—he's going to
> be in town on a gig.

>   JOSIE
> Didn't he do that old Sinatra tune I loved so
> much? What was it . . .

>   SENATOR
>   (sings)
> 'Kings don't mean a thing—on the street of dreams!'

>   JOSIE
> Handsome boy. Good pipes on him.

>   SENATOR
> Used to live out of garbage cans at Zuma.

>   PAIGE
> He's a diehard New Realist—clean and sober a
> long time now. Still does an occasional benefit for
> us.

>   SENATOR
> Chap Starfall. . . . Go and see him, Paige—pull
> him in. Show him the wild blue sky.

EXT. BUILDING OF THE CAPTIVE—NIGHT

The guard lets Josie enter. We hear STARFALL'S version of "Street of Dreams" EMANATING from main house.

INT. BUILDING OF THE CAPTIVE—NIGHT

Josie enters. A shadow-shrouded figure lays in a pristine white bed. A male nurse draws back; Josie sits on bedside chair.

>   JOSIE
> How you feeling?
>   (beat)
> Hungry? Did you eat enough?
>   (beat)
> We never meant to kill your mother. That was so
> many years ago; what's done is done.
>   (beat)
> I loved your father so. . . .

The shrouded figure makes a raspy sound, as if to speak.

>   JOSIE
> What is it?

She turns on small lamp of bedside table. The shrouded figure of course, is Chickie Levitt. He mutters, then clears throat, muttering again. Then:

                                                          (CONTINUED)

CHICKIE
Yis-gadal v'yis-kadash shmei rab—

His bony hand, trembling, reaches for hers as he recites the Jewish Prayer for the Dead . . .

CHICKIE
—b'alma divra khir'utei ve-yamlikh mal-khutei . . .

INT. WILD PALMS—MAIN HOUSE—NIGHT

The STEREO BLASTS "STREET OF DREAMS." The Senator, in a silken robe, twirls a snifter of cognac, singing along:

SENATOR
'Love laughs at a king,
Kings don't mean a thing,
On the Street of Dreams . . . ! Poor?
Nobody's poor,
Long as love is sure—
On the Street of Dreams!'

FADE OUT.

END OF ACT FIVE

ACT SIX

FADE IN:

EXT. HIGHWAY (PCH OR DESERTED)—DAY

Harry and Grace in the 'Vette, on their excursion to the Perceptory, aka "the Resort."

> HARRY
> It's weird you never mentioned this guy. You said he was like an uncle . . .

> GRACE
> I guess some part of me was embarrassed. You know—a prisoner. There's a stigma to even knowing someone like that.

> HARRY
> Does Josie know he's at the Perceptory?

Grace nods.

> HARRY
> Were they close?

> GRACE
> Eli was a visiting professor of American history at the University in Kyoto. Mother took classes there.

> HARRY
> When did he come back to the States?

> GRACE
> I was still really young. When Mother and I moved to L.A., I tried to see him; by then, he was involved with dangerous people. His wife was murdered.

> HARRY
> How long has he been in?

> GRACE
> Twelve or thirteen years.

> HARRY
> (reacts)
> Does he have kids?

> GRACE
> One—I think. A crippled boy.

We HOLD ON Harry, reacting.

(CONTINUED)

They drive onto grounds of nondescript former hotel/spa. Discreet lettering: STATE PERCEPTORY.

INT. PERCEPTORY—DAY

They sit on lobby couch. Casually-dressed employees in Forties and Fifties clothing walk past; Grace is nervous.

> HARRY
> This place isn't really so bad—no wonder they call it the resort. Maybe there's weekend getaway rates for non-offenders. You know, couples.

> GRACE
> Don't even joke about it.

A SMILING WOMAN enters.

> SMILING WOMAN
> Mrs. Wyckoff? Our guest is ready to see you now.

> GRACE
> (to Harry)
> Back in a bit.

> SMILING WOMAN
> (to Harry)
> You're free to walk the grounds. We do ask that visitors wear their badges, and respect posted signs denoting restricted areas.

As they go, Grace looks back at Harry, who makes a face, mocking her guide's overly-cheerful manner.

VISITING ROOM

Grace's led in by Smiling Woman, who then exits. DR. ELI LEVITT stands to greet her; mid-fifties, grey, gaunt, yet athletic—charismatic. A poignant moment; it should be clear they haven't seen each other in a long time. They do not touch.

> ELI
> Hello, Grace.

> GRACE
> Hello. How are you?

> ELI
> All right.

> GRACE
> Every once in awhile, Mother looks at me a certain way—and I know she's seeing you.

(CONTINUED)

ELI

Did you bring Harry?

GRACE
(nods)

I told him you were a friend of the family. I'm . . .
sorry I never visited. All these years—

ELI

You don't have to say it, Grace.

GRACE

I was angry at you for so long—for leaving us.
When I found you again, you pushed me
away . . .

ELI

I was afraid for you. If anything had happened—

GRACE

I know—now. But then, it was just another
rejection. I was barely eighteen. When Josie told
me you were arrested, I was glad. Daddy . . . I'm
so sorry!

ELI

Forgive me—for leaving you alone in that country
with that demonic woman.

Grace takes his hand.

ELI

That is my one—my only—regret. I've lived with
it every day, for over twenty years.

EXT. PERCEPTORY—DAY

Harry exits, walks around building. A man in b.g. steps from car,
with briefcase—Dr. Schenkl. Harry's taking in the mountains when
Schenkl shouts, approaches.

TOBIAS

Harry?

HARRY

Hey, Doc!

TOBIAS
(wagging his finger)

You'd better just be visiting!

HARRY

Nope—finally went over the edge.

(CONTINUED)

                         TOBIAS
You win some, you lose some.

                         HARRY
You're talking about minds, right?

                         TOBIAS
                    (gently chastising)
You haven't been in for a session . . .

                         HARRY
Things have been going too well. No time for
neurosis. I'll try to pencil some in.

                         TOBIAS
Well that's terrific, Harry. I'm happy for you.

                         HARRY
                  (awkward; dissembling)
Grace is visiting an old friend from college—an
alcoholic. What's your excuse?

They begin to walk.

                         TOBIAS
Consulting staff.

                         HARRY
                   (re: conversation)
I'm not being billed for this, am I?

They laugh.

INT. PERCEPTORY—VISITING ROOM—DAY

Grace and her father continue their emotional dialogue; she looks
drawn and fragile.

                         GRACE
I know that the Fathers have done terrible things. I
know that they have taken children from political
enemies; that they have harvested children. What
I need to know, is . . . my son Coty. . . . Is it
possible—I know they consider me one of their
own—they would have to—

                         ELI
What is it, Grace?

                         GRACE
Would they have taken Coty and given me the
son of another? Could they have done that?
Answer me, Father!

EXT. PERCEPTORY—GROUNDS—DAY

                                              (CONTINUED)

Harry and Schenkl walk the grounds near the reflecting pool. Various inmates in colorful (monochrome) outfits stroll past.

> HARRY
> This place is unbelievable. How do they do it?

> TOBIAS
> Drugs, aversion therapy.

> HARRY
> I'm ready!

PAGER GOES OFF.

> TOBIAS
> That's me. Why don't you come in next week—for a tune-up?

> HARRY
> I'll tow myself in for a lube and an ego change.

Schenkl laughs, exits.

EXT. PERCEPTORY—ENTRANCE—DAY

Grace tearfully exits. Harry joins her.

CLOSE on Eli Levitt—fingers twined in chain-link fence. He watches Grace leave building, meet up with Harry; Grace and Harry hug.

> ELI
> (to Self)
> I'll come for you—for all of you. And you will help me, Harry Wyckoff. That's why you were born. . . .

INT. "CHURCH WINDOWS" SET—DAY

Typical sitcom living room, garishly lit. They're taping an episode of "Windows" before a live audience. Coty comes down stairs, in pajamas. Tabba sits on couch, reading.

> COTY
> Mom?

> TABBA
> In here, honey.

> COTY
> I couldn't sleep.

> TABBA
> Poor baby. Let me fix you some warm milk

                    COTY
With a shot of Kahlua?

Audience laughter.

                    TABBA
                    (smiles)
C'mere, you.

He sits beside her; she strokes his head.

                    TABBA
It's a new city . . . new school. Takes getting used
to.

                    COTY
Are you ever gonna get married again?

                    TABBA
                    (tender)
I don't know, Ivan.

                    COTY
Is it 'cause you're still in love with Dad?

                    TABBA
Maybe. It's just hard to meet anyone as wonderful
as your father was.

                    COTY
Is it 'cause Dad was a man of God?

                    TABBA
Not just that.

                    COTY
What about the real estate guy—the one who sold
us the house?

                    TABBA
He was a little crude. Called me a 'fixer-upper.'

Audience laughter.

                    COTY
At least you weren't a 'tear-down.'

Audience laughter.

INT. CHANNEL THREE—HARRY'S OFFICE—DAY

                                          (CONTINUED)

A monitor in the wall of Harry's office runs a tape of the scene we've just been watching. We LOOSEN TO reveal Harry, staring at the drawing of the rhino that Paige gave him. He's interrupted when Jacob, his secretary, enters.

> JACOB
> The Senator wants to see you, Mr. Wyckoff.

> HARRY
> I thought he was in the desert.

> JACOB
> He's here—and you better fasten your seatbelt.
> He's ballistic.

OFFICE OF SENATOR

Harry enters the large, lavish office—with its walls of televisions. The Senator paces, holds handkerchief to nose; heavily congested.

> SENATOR
> Come in, come in, Harry.

> HARRY
> How are you?

> SENATOR
> Mucous-strangled and toxic.

Thrusts papers at him.

> HARRY
> What happened?

> SENATOR
> Injunction: The networks want to stop 'Church Windows'—"W.P.N. has a technological monopoly," blah blah blah. You're damn straight we do! I spent billions earning it!

> HARRY
> I'll have it reversed within 48 hours.

> SENATOR
> Recognize the letterhead? Baum, Weiss and Latimer—your old pals. Thirty years, Harry! I labored thirty years. Now they want to shake the trees and grab all the apples! You're the patent attorney: How does it look?

> HARRY
> (scans papers)
> They're invoking the Paramount Consent Decree.

(CONTINUED)

> SENATOR
> What is it?

> HARRY
> The government forced the studios to sell off their movie theaters—that was in the Forties.
> (scans quotes)
> 'Unlawful . . . MimeCom's unilateral refusal to deal—'

> SENATOR
> MimeCom owns the patent, and I own MimeCom. They're trying to rape me, Harry! It's that friggin' simple!

HARRY'S ANTEROOM/OFFICE

Harry walks briskly past Jacob; he has a plan.

> HARRY
> Jacob, can you come in?

> JACOB
> (following)
> Yes, Mr. Wyckoff?

> HARRY
> I want to arrange a meeting between myself and the networks that filed suit. I want it within 24 hours.

> JACOB
> Shall I inform the Senator's office?

> HARRY
> No.

EXT. CONDOMINIUMS—DAY

Tully Woiwode pulls into the elegant motor court of the Wilshire high-rise.

INT. CONDOMINIUMS—ENTRANCE/LIVING ROOM—DAY

The penthouse apartment of Josie Ito. Woiwode is ushered in by a Japanese houseman and led to couch, where he sits. Josie enters, sweeps regally into room; a palpable animosity between them, like duellists.

> WOIWODE
> Empress! Why oh why didn't I ever do a portrait of you?

JOSIE
Because I won't allow it. You know I don't
approve of likenesses, photographic or otherwise.

WOIWODE
A waste. You're such icon material.

JOSIE
Tell me what you want, Tully—then get out.

Woiwode takes Mazie's broken eyeglasses from his pocket, lays them
on table.

WOIWODE
Give her back to me, Josie. If she's still alive . . .

JOSIE
What are you talking about?

WOIWODE
I hear things—I cover the waterfront, remember?

JOSIE
You cover your ass. You know what? You make
me vomit. You dare come to my home and dictate
to me!

Woiwode suddenly stands, brutally grabbing Josie by the neck. He
smiles, examining her.

WOIWODE
I like you like this—this is a 'you' we don't see
enough of. There's a temple in Toshiba Park,
guarded by a pale, blue-skinned shoki; the eyes
bug out, just like yours.
(tightens grip)
I don't want to play anymore: Can you please get
that through your head, you dried-up monster?
Without Mazie, I am not interested in living! Are
you interested in dying?

She shakes head; he releases grip, goes to door.

WOIWODE
Give her back, or I will send you to a hell you're
not familiar with.

We HOLD ON Josie—gasping, shaken.

INT. WYCKOFF HOUSE—DEN—NIGHT

Harry reads over some contracts in the darkened den. The PHONE
RINGS—he looks surprised that someone's calling so late. He speaks
in hushed tones.

(CONTINUED)

                          HARRY
          When did you get back?
                              (listens)
          Now?
                              (looks at watch)
          It's almost eleven . . .

MASTER BEDROOM

Harry ducks his head in—the TV's ON; Grace is sound asleep. He
exits.

INT. HOLLYWOOD ROOSEVELT—CINEGRILL—NIGHT

Harry enters. A good crowd and an intimate room. CHAP STARFALL
sings onstage, backed by small orchestra.

                          STARFALL
          'There may be trouble ahead
          But while there's moonlight and music and love
          and romance
          Let's face the music and dance . . .'

Harry spots Paige at back booth; slides in next to her—she looks
beautiful. Starfall continues in b.g.

                          PAIGE
          That was fast.

                          HARRY
          Get my phone messages?

                          PAIGE
          They were sweet.

                          HARRY
          Where'd you go?

                          PAIGE
          Kyoto—I thought I told you.

                          HARRY
          No one tells me anything. I missed you.

Waiter appears.

                          HARRY
          Scotch and soda.

Waiter exits.

                          PAIGE
          How's the job going?

                                        (CONTINUED)

                              HARRY
Incredible. I keep pinching myself.

                              PAIGE
                              (flirty)
Can I help with that?

Starfall finishes song to applause. The singer joins them.

                              PAIGE
That was <u>wonderful.</u>

                              HARRY
                         (shakes hand)
Really enjoyed it.

                           STARFALL
Well, thank you.
                              (sits)
We've been having lots of fun. We call it the
'saloon tour'—no amphitheaters or arenas.

                              PAIGE
Chap, this is Harry Wyckoff—Harry's the new
head of business affairs at W.P.N.

                           STARFALL
I've been seeing ads for 'Church Windows.' Wild!

                              HARRY
It's going to change the whole ballgame—I mean,
the way we <u>perceive.</u>

                           STARFALL
That's been the Senator's game plan all along.

                              PAIGE
Chap's a longtime Synthiotics head.

                             HARRY
Before it was chic.

                              PAIGE
The wheel comes 'round.

                           STARFALL
                  (raising glass in toast)
To old love songs . . . and New Realism.

EXT. HOLLYWOOD ROOSEVELT—NIGHT

(CONTINUED)

Paige and Harry emerge; they go well together. A chauffeur scurries
to door of limo, stands in waiting.

                    HARRY
          I wanted to talk to you about your kid. I found out
          some strange information . . .

                    PAIGE
          I have good people working on that now—I
          should have left you out of it.

                    HARRY
          No, listen: Have you ever heard of this group
          called the Fathers?

                    PAIGE
          To do with the government?

                    HARRY
          Remember Tommy Laszlo?

                    PAIGE
          Your crazy friend from college.

                    HARRY
          He was telling me this thing about stolen
          children—some kind of 'recruitment' program.
          Anyone ever mention that to you—I mean,
          anyone who was looking for your kid?

                    PAIGE
          Recruitment for what?

                    HARRY
          I don't know. Probably just his paranoia; he loves
          a conspiracy.

                    PAIGE
          Don't we all?

                    HARRY
          Well—I better get home.

                    PAIGE
          You sure?

                    HARRY
                    (torn)
          Not really. See ya, Paige.
                    (a beat)

                    PAIGE
                    (gets into car)
          'Night, Harry. Dream carefully.

                                        (CONTINUED)

He watches the limo pull away.

                                                                    FADE OUT.

<u>END OF ACT SIX</u>

ACT SEVEN

FADE IN:

INT. WYCKOFF HOUSE—DINING ROOM—NIGHT

Mid-dinner with Harry, Grace, Gavin and Eileen Whitehope; all have been drinking—raucous and merry. Same-sex couples carry on separate conversations.

                    EILEEN
                  (to Grace)
I looked in the toilet and screamed!

                    HARRY
Great title—that's what I'll call my memoirs.

                    GAVIN
Eileen, what the hell are you talking about?

                    EILEEN
Our friends from yoga class . . .

                    GAVIN
                  (to Harry)
I was telling you about those people. . . .

                    GRACE
Your wife has been baring all.

                    GAVIN
Just don't say anything that'll get us into trouble.

                    EILEEN
What was her name, Gavin?

                    GAVIN
Saran—as in Wrap.

                    EILEEN
We've been hearing the sexual stuff for
years—you know, the five-day orgasms—

                    GRACE
Five days? That's got to take some serious
foreplay.

                    EILEEN
No! It all happens without physical contact. They
take this pill they get illegally, from 'The Pharm'—

                    GAVIN
P - H - A - R - M.

(CONTINUED)

> HARRY
> What does all this have to do with a screaming toilet?

> GRACE
> Will you let her finish?

> EILEEN
> This pill they give you turns the water, you know—

> GAVIN
> What Eileen's so discreetly trying to say is, you pee purple.

> HARRY
> You took it?

> GAVIN
> (Stan Laurel)
> We most certainly did.

> GRACE
> I can't take the suspense! What happened?

> EILEEN
> Nothing. They failed to inform us that the first time you take it, there's a delayed response.

> GAVIN
> So, four days later Eileen's in the dentist chair . . .

A beat, then laughter AD LIBS.

INT. LIVING ROOM—LATER

MUSIC: Eileen and Grace struggle through the shag in b.g., a little drunk. Harry and Gavin sit by fire, with drinks—Gavin lights a cigar.

> GAVIN
> It's a gamble, Harry—could blow up in your face. Shouldn't you at least run it by him?

> HARRY
> Too late. Besides, I'm running it by <u>you.</u>

> GAVIN
> I appreciate that.

> HARRY
> I don't know why, but I trust you.

> GAVIN
> I got one question. What are you gonna do when the senator fires your ass?

                              HARRY
                              (beat)
                  Rob a bank. Got any tips?

EXT. VENICE HOME/STUDIO—NIGHT

A Range Rover pulls up under cover of darkness.

INT. VENICE HOME/STUDIO—NIGHT

Tully Woiwode is painting an enormous expressionistic portrait of his sister Mazie. SONNY AND CHER's "I Got You, Babe" BLARES as he works; he occasionally sings along.

INSERT—WIRES AND GLASS

Being carefully cut by black-gloved hands.

INT. VENICE HOME/STUDIO

Woiwode hears something; turns. Goes back to painting. Thinks he hears something again. TURNS MUSIC DOWN—and is immediately seized from behind by hooded men who stuff a gag in his mouth. They pin him to the wall. He struggles, wide-eyed.

Josie makes her entrance. In contrast to the men, she's dressed as if for a cocktail party.

                              JOSIE
                  Sorry we didn't call. I know how much I hate it
                  when people drop by unannounced.

When he sees her, he panics. A third man, behind her, hands her a long glove; she puts it on. She examines Tully's work-in-progress.

                              JOSIE
                  Your work has really improved. It's a wonderful
                  likeness of your sister. You know, if we went to
                  the desert and dug Mazie up, you'd find the
                  resemblance quite amazing. You've captured that
                  "tortured" quality that she had during the last eight
                  or nine hours of the interrogation.

She comes up close. They hold his head against the wall for her.

                              JOSIE
                  Artists have their great periods: Picasso had his
                  Blue—now, Tully Woiwode will have his Blind.

She signals one of the men: he TURNS UP "I GOT YOU BABE" FULL BLAST. Then, Josie holds the artist to her breast and stares at the ceiling while she roughly does what she does to him. On her face, a mixture of empathy, tenderness and strength—the way a mother might hold her child when the child is in pain.

                                        (CONTINUED)

EXT. VENICE HOME/STUDIO—NIGHT

Josie and the men get into Range Rover; Josie discards the long, bloody glove before they exit. We HOLD ON glove a beat, then: a SCREAM. Woiwode staggers out, holding bloody hand to face.

> WOIWODE
> My eyes! The bitch took my eyes!

INT./EXT. CHANNEL THREE—CONFERENCE ROOM/ HALL—DAY

The end of the meeting. Gavin Whitehope approaches conference room as a group of fifteen grim-faced lawyers and TV execs exit. He sees Harry through conference room windows, sleeves rolled up, tie loosened. The last three men file out—a cowed trio: Tom Latimer, Severin Weiss and Morty Winakur.

> WEILL
> Our love to Grace and the kids.

> HARRY
> You bet. Oh, and Morty—next time you go to the
> dry cleaners, have 'em put those little stain
> stickers on the sleeves—that way you'll get out the
> schmutz.

Morty smiles awkwardly, exits. Gavin enters as Harry gets his briefcase together.

> GAVIN
> Capo di tutti capo! How'd it go?

> HARRY
> They went for it—had to.

> GAVIN
> What a big genius you are. When are you going
> to tell the old man?

> HARRY
> I'm on my way to the desert right now.

> GAVIN
> Did you know it was his birthday?

> HARRY
> How's his mood?

> GAVIN
> Good. Upbeat; vengeful. Now, come on. We
> gotta get over to the media room—they got the
> 'Windows' demo set up.

> HARRY
> Now?

                    GAVIN
        You won't <u>believe</u> it.

They exit into hall.

INT. MEDIA ROOM

A facsimile of a typical home media room, Harry settles into couch,
facing television. There's a small, sleek "cable"-type box sitting on top
TV. A few technicians move IN and OUT OF FRAME. Gavin AD
LIBS to them re: demo readiness.

                    HARRY
        How many adaptors have we sold?

                    GAVIN
        Radio Shack's done about twenty million
        units—the response has been phenomenal.

                    HARRY
        I had this <u>unbelievable</u> experience at the beach. I
        put on a pair of glasses—this <u>ballroom</u> suddenly—

                    GAVIN
        We got rid of the glasses—too many glitches.
        Those will only be used for total
        immersion—custom stuff. Not everyone can afford
        it, anyway.

                    HARRY
        Tell me about the box.

                    GAVIN
        That's the adaptor—just like for cable, only it's a
        computer that generates synthetic holograms: Your
        TV scans the room, infrared—<u>knows</u> where you're
        sitting, <u>knows</u> where the couch and chairs are.
        There's even a collision detector—optional.

The lights dim and Tabba is suddenly sitting beside Harry on the
couch. Unlike the feverish reality of Chickie Levitt's ballroom, this
one is scarily mundane—more real. Harry AD LIBS amazement. Coty
enters from behind a smiling Gavin.

                    COTY
        I couldn't sleep.

                    TABBA
        Poor baby. Let me fix you some warm milk . . .

                    COTY
        With a shot of Kahlua?

Deafening AUDIENCE LAUGHTER—Harry winces, covers ears.
Gavin shouts to off-screen technician.

                                    (CONTINUED)

> GAVIN
> Can we lower volume?

It LOWERS. Harry reaches out to touch Tabba—she moves away.

> GAVIN
> Collision detector.

> HARRY
> This is too weird!

While scene plays out, Harry stands, moves around them, scrutinizing Coty and Tabba from various angles.

> COTY
> What about the real estate guy—the one who sold us the house?

> TABBA
> He was a little crude. Called me a 'fixer-upper.'

Harry laughs along with the AUDIENCE, exhilarated.

> GAVIN
> Ready to go interactive? It's another custom program—won't be ready for at least a year.
> Touch her.

Harry reaches out gingerly, touching Tabba from behind; his finger goes through her to the first joint. Nothing happens.

> TECHNICIAN (O.S.)
> Try again, Mr. Wyckoff.

He does. This time, to his total amazement, Tabba turns around and seems to stare into his eyes.

> TABBA
> Let me fix you some warm milk. Poor baby. Poor baby. Poor baby. Poor baby. Poor baby. Poor—

INT. WYCKOFF HOUSE—MASTER BEDROOM—DAY

Grace is in bed, in her nightgown, doing a jigsaw—this one is circular, and all black. The TV's on, MOS.

> JOSIE (O.S.)
> Grace?

Enters, out of breath.

> JOSIE
> There you are. Criminy—can't climb those stairs anymore. Are you sick?

(CONTINUED)

Grace ignores her, re: puzzle.

                    JOSIE
     What is that?

                    GRACE
     The black hole.
                    (ironic)
     Thought you'd recognize it.

                    JOSIE
     Lovely.

                    GRACE
                    (beat)
     I went to see Daddy.

                    JOSIE
                    (feigned cool)
     Really. Is he well?

                    GRACE
     Tell me about the Fathers. Tell me what you
     know—about the abduction of children.

                    JOSIE
     It was a way to strike at men who were out to
     burn the very fabric of our nation—of our world.
     If the children of our enemies could join us, and
     move against their own, this would be a great gift.
     That was the thinking, anyway.

                    GRACE
     How far did it go, Mother?

                    JOSIE
     I don't think I know what you mean.

                    GRACE
     Who decided? Who decided which children
     would be taken?

                    JOSIE
     I already told you . . .

                    GRACE
     Was it you and the Senator?

                    JOSIE
     We didn't sanction any of it!

                    GRACE
     Liar!

                                        (CONTINUED)

Grace stands, upsetting the puzzle—it falls to the floor in pieces. She grabs her mother.

> GRACE
> I just want to know one thing: Who is that little boy—the one I've called my own?

> JOSIE
> (backs away from her)
> You're insane—just like Eli Levitt!

> GRACE
> (moves on her)
> You tell me, Mother—I want to know! Who is that little boy! And what did they do to my baby?

EXT. WILD PALMS—LIVING ROOM—DUSK

Harry awaits the Senator. THROUGH the windows, the trees swirl in the wind. Kreutzer enters, in tuxedo pants and suspenders; shirtless. He's running an ice cube over his chest.

> SENATOR
> I'm either too hot or too cold—all the damned time.

> HARRY
> Happy birthday.

> SENATOR
> Did you get me something good?

> HARRY
> I talked to the networks today. I got you a deal.

> SENATOR
> I don't think I heard you right.

> HARRY
> I settled the suit. I think you'll be happy with—

> SENATOR
> (hurls a vase)
> You sonofabitch! You dare dealing with those half-heads behind my back?

> HARRY
> Listen to me! You've spent 40 years preparing for this moment, 40 years a visionary—<u>act like one</u>! You've <u>got</u> to sell the technology—

> SENATOR
> I told you, never!

(CONTINUED)

> HARRY
>
> Can't you see they'll get hold of it anyway? This isn't some recipe for chili—it's only a matter of time before someone does it and does it better. Let 'em have it! At least that way, you retain some control.

> SENATOR
> (calming)
> You made a deal?

> HARRY
>
> In ten months' time, we will agree to license the technology, for which we will collect a royalty, in perpetuum, the likes of nothing that anyone has ever dreamed. By then, it won't matter if there are a thousand networks. In the eyes of the world, there will only be Channel Three.

The Senator begins to laugh; roars. Harry relaxes.

> SENATOR
> Behind my back!

INT. BLDG OF CAPTIVE

Chap Starfall sits beside the fragile Chickie, who eats a meal off a tray that swivels over his bed. Chap wears a tux, as if he's on his way to a gig; helps Chickie cut his food.

> CHICKIE
> Where are my things?

> STARFALL
> They're safe. Everything was moved; it's all here now.

> CHICKIE
> They want me to tell them secrets. They want to know about the GO chip.

> STARFALL
> You know what Synthiotics calls 'The Last Secret'? That there are no secrets anymore.

> CHICKIE
> The Senator wants to be immortal. . . .

> STARFALL
> Could anyone be more deserving?

> CHICKIE
> There's someone I need to talk to.

(CONTINUED)

                            STARFALL
Who's that?

                            CHICKIE
A girl.
                    (embarrassed)
Her name is . . . Terra.

EXT. MALIBU BEACH HOUSE—DUSK

Harry and Paige walk along beach.

                            HARRY
I saw 'Church Windows' today.

                            PAIGE
It's only the beginning. Why should <u>this</u> reality be
public domain? What's so great about it? Tony
wants a new, <u>improved</u> reality, controlled by
MimeCom and sold straight out of Seven-Eleven!

                            HARRY
I'm glad I found you again.

                            PAIGE
It's all there, for the taking—a world where we
don't have to be afraid to leave our dreams open
at night.

He kisses her, hard; drags her onto sand, pulling her down into his
arms.

                            HARRY
You make me feel like there aren't any limits—

                            PAIGE
They found the man who took my son.

                            HARRY
Where?

                            PAIGE
They're bringing him in. They want me to be
there—to identify him. I'm scared, Harry! Will you
be there? Will you be with me?

                            HARRY
If you want me to—

                            PAIGE
I want you. I need you . . .

                            HARRY
I'll be there.

                                                    (CONTINUED)

                              PAIGE
            You'll come?

                              HARRY
            I'll come, Paige.

                              PAIGE
            You'll come with me?

                              HARRY
            Yes . . .

                              PAIGE
            Come with me, Harry. I want you to come—

The waves crash over them as they embrace.

EXT. WYCKOFF HOUSE—MASTER BEDROOM—NIGHT

Grace drinks and cries—surrounded by photographs. CAMERA PANS
TO photo: Grace, in hospital, joyously holding her "lost" newborn.

DEIRDRE'S ROOM

Coty and Deirdre look out the window. They see the Maps to the
Stars Boy staring up at them from back yard. WIND BLOWS the
trees.

INT. HOSPITAL—NIGHT

Tully Woiwode gets up from his bed, goes to window. His eyes are
bandaged. He slides window open so he can feel the Santa Anas on
his face.

INT. BLDG OF CAPTIVE—NIGHT

Chickie wears his special glasses. He does a pantomime, as if he is
dancing with someone—though we can't see her, we know it's Terra.

INT. WILD PALMS—NIGHT

The Senator gathers with Josie and Tabba and Starfall. They hold
their glasses in a toast.

                              ALL
            The palm at the end of the mind, beyond the last
            thought, rises/In the bronze decor . . .

They drink, then a servant hands the Senator a huge knife: The
Senator cuts through a cake in the form of stained-glass church
windows.

EXT. BEACH—DAY

PERCUSSIVE MUSIC. INTERCUT victim in dune buggy flying over sand, chased by two Range Rovers. A silent chopper's white beam jaggedly illuminates the scene. INTERCUT Paige and Harry, in back seat of lead Rover. Harry's excited, but a little confused—he shouts to her above the action.

> HARRY
> I can't believe we're chasing this guy!

> PAIGE
> We're gonna nail him—

> HARRY
> (indicates men in front seat)
> Are they the police?

> PAIGE
> Special units—they call them 'Watchers.'

The buggy spins out in water. The victim jumps, runs along shore. The lead Rover stops; Paige jumps out, pulls gun from jacket—Harry notes this with some alarm.

> PAIGE
> Come on!

> HARRY
> Wait a minute—

She chases victim, with Harry running after her. The men in the Rovers seem to disappear—it's Paige and Harry vs. the victim. As they gain on him, Paige falls, twisting ankle. Harry stops.

> PAIGE
> (hands him gun)
> Take him—

> HARRY
> Take him where?

> PAIGE
> Don't let him get away, Harry! Not now—

> HARRY
> But I don't—I don't know who he is!

> PAIGE
> Dammit, he took my son! He's a killer of
> children! What more do you need to know?
> Please, Harry!

> HARRY
> (frozen)
> What am I doing? I can't shoot anybody!

(CONTINUED)

                                  PAIGE
They're rubber bullets—to stun . . .

                                  HARRY
                    (looks around for police, baffled)
                    What happened to the men?

                                  PAIGE
                                (scathing)
You're just a poor little lawyer, who lost his way
home. You don't care about anyone or anything
but <u>yourself</u>!

Harry bolts, throwing himself into it. We TRACK WITH him as he
chases victim over sand—a hard run. Harry falls, losing gun in
darkness. Paige's FADING SCREAMS urge him on. Harry gains on
quarry; the exhausted runners move slower now. A final burst of
energy—Harry accelerates, tackles. They grapple in darkness. Harry
connects, knocking man out. Harry turns him over and gasps.

                                  HARRY
            Oh God, no!
                                  (beat)
            Tommy!

CLOSE ON TOMMY

Wet, bruised and barely conscious, his hand reaches for Harry,
clutching, eyes half-open.

                                  TOMMY
                    Woi—wode . . . Woi—wode . . .

                                  HARRY
            Tommy . . .

Tommy brings his mouth to Harry's ear, whispering hoarsely.

                                  TOMMY
                    <u>This is how it begins.</u>

Passes out in Harry's arms.

                                                    FADE TO BLACK.

END CREDITS

OVER a row of palms, blown by wild winds:

                                  STARFALL (V.O.)
                    <u>'There may be trouble ahead . . .</u>
                    <u>But while there's moonlight and music and love</u>
                    <u>and romance</u>
                    <u>Let's face the music and dance!</u>'

                              <u>THE END</u>

WILD PALMS

Third Hour

"The Floating World"

ACT ONE

FADE IN:

EXT. PACIFIC DESIGN CENTER—CHANNEL THREE—DAY

PAIGE KATZ exits hurriedly from Channel Three; Harry appears moments after, in pursuit. A limo, as yet unrevealed, is parked at the curb of the vast entrance.

> HARRY
>
> Paige!
> (she turns)
> Why didn't you return my calls?

> PAIGE
>
> I was out of town—an emergency. What is it?
> What's going on?

> HARRY
>
> I need to talk about Tommy.

> PAIGE
>
> Drop it, Harry! It's done!

> HARRY
>
> I can't drop it, Paige! He's my closest friend!

> PAIGE
>
> Your closest friend took my little boy away from
> me!

> HARRY
>
> You keep saying that, but I can't—

> PAIGE
> (beat, then)
> He was in love with me.

> HARRY
> (stunned)
> Tommy?

> PAIGE
>
> The night you introduced us, he hit on me,
> heavily.

> HARRY
>
> I don't believe it.

(CONTINUED)

> PAIGE
I thought he was just loaded and being funny—Harry's 'wild man' best friend. He was pretty out of control. A year later, you and I were fighting; you said some terrible things to me. Tommy came over. We got drunk . . .

> HARRY
I'll wing the rest.
> (stung)
The omnivorous Paige Katz . . .

> PAIGE
It never happened again. When you and I broke up, Tommy thought I'd want to be with him. He became obsessed—even started working for the Senator, to be near me.

> HARRY
Tommy worked for the Senator?

> PAIGE
> (nods)
Rose to First Tier, Synthiotics. They caught him trying to steal MimeCom software—broke the Senator's heart. That's when Tommy joined the Friends.
> (re: her betrayal)
I'm sorry, Harry.

> HARRY
I still don't—why did he take your son?

> PAIGE
Revenge. Because he couldn't have me. The Friends said it was political—a retaliation against the Senator and his people.
> (shakes her head)
Peter's kidnapping was an act of personal terrorism and nothing more.

> HARRY
'The Senator and his people?'

> PAIGE
The Fathers.
> (Harry's nonplussed)
The Senator founded the Fathers. I thought you knew . . .

She breaks away.

> HARRY
Paige, wait—

(CONTINUED)

We HOLD ON Harry, taking it all in.

INT. MEDIA ROOM—DAY

Harry sits on the couch of a darkened room. GAVIN walks over with two drinks; hands Harry a glass.

> HARRY
> (impatient)
> Gav, I gotta pile of work that's gotta be handled before the 'Windows' debut. What did you want me down here for?

> GAVIN
> A little demo.

> HARRY
> I've seen the damn demo.

> GAVIN
> Not this, you haven't. We're gonna add a little twist.

> HARRY
> Like what?

> GAVIN
> Like, drink this.

> HARRY
> What is it?

> GAVIN
> Mimezine—aka 'Pharm Juice.' It's experimental.

> HARRY
> From your yoga friends, right?

> GAVIN
> (nods)
> True media freaks, what can I say?

> HARRY
> I don't know about this. What exactly is it?

> GAVIN
> An empathigen, brewed up by a couple of rogue neuropharmacologists. Only lasts two minutes.

> HARRY
> What are the side effects?

> GAVIN
> Just one: It'll change your life.

(CONTINUED)

                         HARRY
No delayed dental chair orgasms?

                         GAVIN
Not as long as you floss.

                         HARRY
I don't think we should be doing this at work.
Maybe I'll try it on the weekend—

                         GAVIN
Would you stop being such a prude? Where's
your sense of adventure?

                         HARRY
Does anyone know?

                         GAVIN
Nobody knows. Now drink.

                         HARRY
      (after a beat, Harry swallows his drink)
Now what.

                         GAVIN
                    (sings)
'Purple haze, all in my brain'! Are you
experienced, Harry?

                         HARRY
Can you be serious for a minute?

                         GAVIN
''Scuse me, while I kiss the sky'!
         (EXITS FRAME as room darkens)
Hope you like Wagner—

MUSIC from "PARSIFAL." A BEAUTY PAGEANT WINNER in swimsuit
materializes before Harry. She is Japanese and wears a ribbon from
shoulder to hip: Miss Alabama. She holds a bouquet of roses in her
hands—Gavin watches the delighted Harry from the wings.

                     BEAUTY QUEEN
May I talk to you a moment?

                         GAVIN
You're the beauty show judge—say something,
stupid!

                         HARRY
           (awkward, to Beauty Queen)
Hello . . .

                                                    (CONTINUED)

> BEAUTY QUEEN
> I . . . I just wanted to thank you personally for
> your vote, Judge.

She plucks a rose from bouquet and hands one to Harry; he holds it, puzzled—it seems to be "real."

> HARRY
> Gavin, what _is_ this?

> GAVIN
> The Mimezine—it's flooding your cerebral cortex!

> BEAUTY QUEEN
> (moving closer)
> I saw the way you looked at me onstage. I wanted
> you to touch me . . .

Harry laughs nervously—he doesn't quite believe what he's experiencing.

> GAVIN
> Go ahead! The adaptor's tracking your hands—
> the Mimezine'll give you the illusion of touch.

Harry slowly extends his hand and "caresses" her cheek. The Beauty Queen sighs, and puts her hand atop Harry's: He clearly feels something there.

> BEAUTY QUEEN
> You made me queen of the pageant: Now I'll
> make you king . . . with my mouth.

> GAVIN
> Go for it, Harry!

She leans to him, kissing him on the lips.

> GAVIN
> Yes! Yes! We have contact! Yes!

INT. WYCKOFF HOUSE—BATHROOM

Harry, still in shirt and tie, sits across from Grace as she soaks in tub. Only a candle glows.

> HARRY
> It was the _weirdest_ thing I've _ever_ experienced.

> GRACE
> Was it _legal,_ what he gave you?

(CONTINUED)

                    HARRY
Mimezine? It's not even classified yet. Works on
the lower brain—the reticular something-
something. They're tapping into some kind of
primordial, cortical weirdness. What they've been
talking about is true, Grace: It _is_ a new reality . . .

                    GRACE
Hail, Synthiotics!

She nods out.

                    HARRY
Hey, what's the matter?

                    GRACE
Just tired, I guess . . .

                    HARRY
You been drinking, Grace?

                    GRACE
A little vermouth: It helps me with my diary of a
mad housewife. I feel very 'twenties' lately—very
Zelda Fitzgerald. I'm a flapper, without fins . . .

                    HARRY
Let's dry you off.

                    GRACE
Just a while longer. . . . Tell me more about your
little "tryst."

                    HARRY
A lovestruck beauty pageant queen—I'm telling
you, it was _pure soap._

                    GRACE
Does bring a whole new spin to infidelity. Let's be
scientific, may we? If you had to compare the way
she kissed—

                    HARRY
It wasn't really a _kiss._ It's a _head_ thing—

                    GRACE
I know, I know—cortical. But just for argument's
sake: How would she rate next to, say . . . Paige
Katz?

                    HARRY
                 (steely)
There isn't anything between Paige and me.

                                    (CONTINUED)

> GRACE
> (laughs)
> Nothing but blood and tissue and hot, hot tears.
> (beat)
> 'Scuse me while I slip into a warm coma . . .

> HARRY
> Grace? Grace . . .

He turns on the light switch—Grace is soaking in a bloody bubble bath. Harry rushes to her.

EXT. STREETS—NIGHT

An AMBULANCE SCREAMS through the streets, revolving blue light flashing.

INT. BEVERLY CLINIC—GRACE'S ROOM—NIGHT

Grace lays in bed, sedated, with bandaged wrists. Harry sits beside her. A soft wind blows in from sliding door that leads to terrace. She mutters—in Japanese. Then:

> GRACE
> You know what Japan is, Harry? A pretty little girl who throws up to stay thin. Post-suicidal musings, by Grace Wyckoff. . . . When I was little, Mama used to take me to Hiroshima for kabuki. There was one about this deformed princess—born with her hand in a fist. Someone turned her into a whore . . .

> HARRY
> Why did you do it, Grace?

> GRACE
> Why? Because we like you.
> (beat)
> I feel like an animal that knows it's going to die . . .
>   (as she traces her bandage with a finger)
> Full of ghosts, kabuki. Always loved the ghosts; never scared me.
> (beat)
> They scare me now, Harry. They scare me now.

EXT. WYCKOFF HOUSE—BACK YARD—MORNING

Harry slides open glass door, staring toward pool with consternation. He's still in his pajamas. CAMERA REVEALS two men standing in the empty shallow end of the pool: Gavin Whitehope and STITCH WALKEN.

> HARRY
> Gavin? What's happening?

(CONTINUED)

>   GAVIN
>   Sorry to hear about Grace. Can we show you
>   something a minute?

He waves his fingers, signaling Harry to come closer. Harry's a bit
tentative, vaguely threatened by the incongruous visit.

>   GAVIN
>   Meet Stitch Walken—the stand-up.

>   STITCH
>   I just flew in from the Perceptory—and boy, is my
>   mind tired!

>   GAVIN
>   You've probably seen him on cable; <u>hilarious.</u>

They begin to walk Harry toward the deep end.

>   HARRY
>   Mind telling me what's going on?

>   STITCH
>   Who are you, Marvin Gaye?
>   (sings)
>   'What's goin' on' . . .

>   GAVIN
>   Stitch does this bit about the laundry—do it,
>   Stitch! Do the bit!

>   STITCH
>   My relationship was in the toilet: The old lady and
>   I were fighting all the time . . .
>   (beat)
>   Mom finally threw me out!
>   (as Gavin cracks up)
>   For the first time in my life, I had to do my own
>   laundry. Took three months—all the clothes said
>   'wash separately.'

>   GAVIN
>   (guffaws, to Harry)
>   Do you love it?

They reach drain at deep end. Stitch kneels, opening a trapdoor: The
stairs lead to blackness.

>   HARRY
>   What is this, Gavin? Am I dreaming?

>   GAVIN
>   No—it's okay. You're fine . . .

                                STITCH
                          (a la W.C. Fields)
                Down, down, down—through the pool of tears!

The men go down. Gavin's the last.

INT. ROOMS BENEATH POOL—DAY

More stairs and dampness. They reach corridor at bottom, then Stitch
hits a switch marked "FLOOD."

EXT. BACK YARD—DAY

The pool begins filling up.

INT. ROOMS BENEATH POOL—DAY

A large sign on wall reads: NO LIFEGUARD ON DUTY. Harry
Wyckoff is tied to a chair. Sitting in a semi-circle around him are the
blind Tully Woiwode, Gavin and Stitch. The scene should be played
rapid-fire, Harry weathering the verbal assault.

                                WOIWODE
                Welcome, Harry.

                                HARRY
                What the hell is all this?

                                GAVIN
                These are the tunnels the Friends built.

                                STITCH
                And these are the hands that dug the tunnels—

                                WOIWODE
                And these were the eyes that watched the hands
                that dug—

                                HARRY
                What happened to you?

                                WOIWODE
                Had a makeover.
                          (removes sunglasses)
                Josie and I put our heads together—came up with
                a whole new 'look.'

                                STITCH
                Does have its advantages—you'll never be
                'designated driver' again.

                                HARRY
                Someone tell me what the hell is going on!

                                                          (CONTINUED)

                         WOIWODE
Sorry about tying you up—we had to, or you
wouldn't listen.

                          GAVIN
Anything to eat around here?

                         WOIWODE
Still having the visions, Harry?

                          GAVIN
The rhino's key, Harry. We all saw the rhino.

                         STITCH
Not everyone sees the rhino.

                          GAVIN
I would kill for some onion soup.

                         WOIWODE
Lose your self-importance: No one cares about
Harry Wyckoff. You think the Senator cares?

                          HARRY
Look: I'm not interested in anything political. Let
me go, Gavin. I have a family . . .

                          GAVIN
You mean a semblance of a family—

                         WOIDODE
The Depression this country went through was
planned, Harry. And the Florida bomb?

                          GAVIN
Ninety thousand dead—

                         WOIWODE
Know what one of our Southern senators called it?

                         STITCH
A 'cotton burn-off'—controlled fire.

                         WOIWODE
No terrorists involved, Harry—strictly government.
Boca Raton was a premeditated nuclear event that
conferred extraordinary new powers on the police.

                         STITCH
The Liberty Bill—textbook stuff.

                         WOIWODE
Within two years, the Friends were
decimated—murdered or locked up in desert
'hospitals.'

                                        (CONTINUED)

                    GAVIN
Wake up, Harry—you're having a very important
nightmare.

                    HARRY
Why are you telling me this?

                    STITCH
Wanna wind up like Tommy?

                    HARRY
What happened to him? Where is he?

                    WOIWODE
At the Perceptory—they're dosing him with
Mimezine. . . .

                    HARRY
No!

                    STITCH
It wasn't your fault. You were just along for the
ride . . .

                    WOIWODE
We're the shock troops of reality, Harry, don t you
understand?

                    STITCH
Go see Grace's father—Eli Levitt. Smart man.

                    HARRY
                (another shock)
Her _father_?

                    GAVIN
Didn't you know that, Harry?

                    STITCH
                (light)
Even _I_ knew that. My _mother-in-law_ knew that.
Your marriage was arranged, Harry. Coty isn't
your son—he was conceived at a Synthiotics
house in upstate New York and delivered in a
bungalow at the Beverly Hills Hotel. Bought-and-
sold property of the Fathers. That much we know.

                    WOIWODE
Help us, Harry! Think about where you came
from. I know you've been trying to remember.
Think . . .

                    STITCH
Think—

GAVIN
Think!

CAMERA PUSHES IN ON Harry as the ECHO assaults him.

EXT. WYCKOFF HOUSE—BACK YARD—DAY

COTY wanders to edge of pool, staring into the water enigmatically as the pool continues to fill.

FADE OUT.

END OF ACT ONE

ACT TWO

FADE IN:

INT. THERAPIST'S OFFICE—DAY

Harry on the couch at DR. SCHENKL'S.

> HARRY
> They said Grace and I are living in an old safe
> house—from the early days of the Movement.
> There's this huge network of tunnels, like a
> subway for paranoids.

> TOBIAS
> And where did you surface?

> HARRY
> I was blindfolded; somewhere near the beach.
> They said Tommy was at the Perceptory. . . . I
> haven't had a chance to drain the pool, to see if it
> was just a dream.

> TOBIAS
> You've been under stress; Grace's hospitalization
> hasn't helped—

> HARRY
> They said crazy things about my marriage—about
> my son. . . . Sick as it sounds, I wish I'd seen the
> rhino. At least then, I'd know it was a dream.

> TOBIAS
> Have you talked to Gavin about what happened?

> HARRY
> We're having lunch. What the hell am I going to
> say? 'Hey, Gavin, was that you at the Twilight
> Zone pool party?' I'll feel him out. One thing is
> comforting: He's crazy as I am . . .

EXT. STREETS—DAY

Driving through Hollywood, Gavin passes a billboard: THEY SAID
THE REVOLUTION WOULDN'T BE TELEVISED. THEY WERE
WRONG. "CHURCH WINDOWS"—COMING, ON WPN.

He drives on; sees a boy wearing sandwich boards advertising Maps
to the Stars—the boy frantically waves him town. Gavin stops as boy
runs to car, leaning in window—it's Coty.

> COTY
> Help me! They're chasing me—

(CONTINUED)

                                    GAVIN
                              (throws open door)
                    Get in!

INT. GAVIN'S CAR—DAY

As they drive, Gavin takes a closer look. A tattoo peeks through
Coty's shirt—just like the other boy.

                                    COTY
                              (still breathless)
                    Thanks, mister—

                                    GAVIN
                    Wait a minute—you're Coty Wyckoff!

                                    COTY
                    How do you know my name?

                                    GAVIN
                    I met you at the house. I work with your dad at
                    Channel Three.

                                    COTY
                    They want to kill me!

                                    GAVIN
                    Who wants to kill you? What are you doing out
                    here—with those maps?

                                    COTY
                    Peter called—said he was in trouble . . .

                                    GAVIN
                    Peter?

                                    COTY
                    You know who Peter is—that's why you stopped;
                    you thought I was him.

                                    GAVIN
                    How do you know him?

                                    COTY
                    He came to my school last year. He said we had
                    a lot in common.

                                    GAVIN
                    Those tattoos—

                                    COTY
                    It's only paint.

                                    GAVIN
                    Why?

                                                        (CONTINUED)

> COTY
> Peter said I had to make it look like it was
> him . . .

> GAVIN
> Where is he?

EXT. IVAR TERRACE MOTEL—DAY

Gavin perspires heavily as they climb outside stairs of motel. Next to
the VACANCY sign is another: COLOR TV/WE HAVE
MIMADAPTORS! They stop at room Coty indicates. Gavin knocks;
no answer. Gavin tries door—it's open.

INT. IVAR MOTEL—DAY

They enter the seedy room. Gavin looks around—nothing. As he
turns back, Coty fells him with some kind of electrical
stunner—Gavin falls to the bed, twitching. Coty is eerily calm and
polite. He sits on bed beside paralyzed executive.

> COTY
> I'm really sorry—that's not supposed to hurt, by
> the way. It wears off. I just wanted to talk to you. I
> made up the stuff about Peter being here.

Throughout scene, Coty fingers tattoo beneath his shirt and gently
"fingerpaints" Gavin's face.

> COTY
> This is a hard time for us—exciting, but hard. I'm
> sure you know about Mother being in the
> hospital; there's lots of pressure on Dad,
> too—'Windows,' the new job. . . . Everyone thinks
> he's doing pretty great though. It's just extra hard
> when the Friends tell him a bunch of stuff that
> isn't true.

Men arrive outside room; we see their silhouettes on curtains. Coty
takes out small case. Gavin follows all of this with his eyes, and
becomes agitated—he quakes and makes throat-noises.

> COTY
> You know what's funny to think about? You love
> food so much. But you're never ever going to eat
> again. Not even an egg, or a strawberry, or a little
> pea. They're going to come in soon and ask you
> about Peter; it won't be so bad.
> (removes scalpel from case; as Gavin quakes again)
> They showed me how, but I'm nervous.
> (giggles; beat)
> I'm going to do some cutting now, okay?

INT. PRIVATE PSYCHIATRIC—GRACE'S ROOM—DAY

(CONTINUED)

Grace sits on the bed, packing her things. Peter, the
Maps to the Stars Boy, wanders in.

> GRACE
> Hi, there.

> PETER
> Hi.

> GRACE
> Are you visiting someone?

> PETER
> My mother.

> GRACE
> What's your name?

> PETER
> Peter.

> GRACE
> I'm Grace.

> PETER
> Did they put you in a bathtub with a cover and a
> little hole to stick your head through?

> GRACE
> (amused)
> Not that I know of.

> PETER
> That's what they did to Olivia de Havilland, in
> Snakepit. I have her house on my map—the place
> she used to live. May I see the terrace?

Grace is charmed, baffled and intrigued all at once. Who is this boy?
Why does he pull her? As Peter exits, the same Nurse enters.

> NURSE
> The eagle has landed.

> GRACE
> My mother?

> NURSE
> You're going home in style—she brought a limo.

> GRACE
> Be right there.

The Nurse exits. Grace goes to sliding glass door, moves aside
curtain. The boy is gone.

(CONTINUED)

GRACE
Peter?

EXT. WILD PALMS—TERRACE/ROCK GARDEN—DAY

We TRACK WITH Harry and Paige as they approach terrace and pool area.

PAIGE
I told you, Tommy's at Central Jail.

HARRY
That's not what I heard, Paige. Anyway, I called—they have no record of a Tony Laszlo.

PAIGE
We'll talk about it later. . . .

They arrive at a large, rectangular garden composed of gravel and five or six rocks of varying sizes.

HARRY
Beautiful. It's for meditation?

PAIGE
Uh huh. Tell me what you see—you know, like a Rorschach.

HARRY
What is this, Zen Freudism?

PAIGE
People usually say 'islands in the sea, mountains in the clouds . . .'

HARRY
(a beat, then)
Dogs in the water, maybe?

PAIGE
(laughs)
Dogs in the water!

HARRY
You know, paddling. See? The rocks look like little heads in the water.
(as she still laughs)
Did I fail the serenity test?

The Senator enters from house, in a gorgeous Japanese-style silk robe. He's pumped up—like he just had a shower and a workout.

SENATOR
Harry, Harry, how does my garden grow?

(CONTINUED)

                         HARRY
Incredible. Beautiful—I love it.

                         SENATOR
Recognize it?

                         HARRY
                         (doesn't)
It's a—a Zen garden . . .

                         SENATOR
The Zen garden—

                         PAIGE
Ryoanji, in Kyoto.

                         SENATOR
Faithful to the centimeter.

                         PAIGE
Harry said it looks like dogs in the water.

                         HARRY
I was kidding.

                         SENATOR
I love that.

                         HARRY
Then I wasn't kidding.

                         SENATOR
'He looked at Ryoanji and saw dogs in the water.'
That's kickass haiku!

                         PAIGE
Anton was going to have the real thing brought
over, stone by stone.

                         HARRY
Seriously?

                         SENATOR
Damn right. Knew some yakuza who'd steal the
whole damn garden for me.

                         HARRY
They never recovered the Pieta.

                         SENATOR
                         (looks out at garden)
Fell in love the first time I saw it. That was thirty
years ago. I'm sitting there, looking at this . . .
perfect thing—when suddenly I hear a voice on
                         (MORE)

                                                     (CONTINUED)

> SENATOR (CONT'D)
> the loudspeaker: 'There is no serenity to equal that
> of Ryoanji.' For the tourists—over and over.

> HARRY
> The white zone is for loading and unloading
> only—

> PAIGE
> This is the part of the story where you're supposed
> to say you achieved enlightenment.

> SENATOR
> I sure did. See, that's the world now—eternity's
> just another ride at Euro-Disney.
> (walks toward house)
> You're going to Kyoto—both of you. Right after
> 'Windows' debuts.

> HARRY
> Why?

> SENATOR
> There's something I want you to pick up—part of
> the 'Go' game. You've played Go, haven't you,
> Harry?

> HARRY
> As in, 'everything must'?

> SENATOR
> (laughs; exits)
> Paige is a helluva guide. She'll show you the
> tao— I'm not talkin' Dow Jones!

INT. WYCKOFF HOUSE—DINING ROOM—NIGHT

The debut of "Church Windows." Harry, Grace, JOSIE and the kids
are finishing dinner.

Josie helps Deirdre with her food; Coty can barely sit still.

> GRACE
> (somber)
> When did they find him?

> HARRY
> A few days ago—in the Angeles National Forest.

> COTY
> Grammie, how many people are watching the
> show?

(CONTINUED)

                              JOSIE
'Bout three drillion—and they <u>all</u> want to see Coty
Wyckoff.

                              GRACE
It just doesn't make any sense. . . .

                              COTY
                          (to Grace)
You're not going to get depressed, are you?

                              HARRY
Don't be smart, Coty.

                              COTY
I wasn't being smart.

                              GRACE
                          (to Harry)
It's all right.
                          (to Coty)
I'm not depressed, darling.

                              JOSIE
It's awful—I hope they catch whoever's
responsible.

                              HARRY
One of Gavin's kids is a cop . . . maybe it was
some kind of retaliation.

                              JOSIE
Is this suitable dinner talk?

                              COTY
What time is it? What time is it?

                              JOSIE
You know, little guy, you're worse than Christmas
morning. Can we excuse this perpetual-motion
machine from the table?

                              GRACE
Coty, go ahead and take your sister.

Coty and Deirdre exit.

                              HARRY
I'm glad <u>he's</u> excited—<u>I'm</u> about to heave.

                              GRACE
Why don't we go away for a coupla days. We can
go up the coast, to Big Sur. . . .

(CONTINUED)

> HARRY
> Maybe when I get back—the Senator wants me in Kyoto.

> GRACE
> When?

> HARRY
> Wednesday morning.

> GRACE
> I'll go with you. . . .

> JOSIE
> (exiting)
> Don't be desperate, darling. You're just getting on your feet again—the last thing you want is travel.

> GRACE
> (coy)
> Maybe I should come along. . . .

> HARRY
> It's business, Grace. I'm literally going to be there forty-eight hours.

> GRACE
> Oh, come on, Harry: I'll be incognito—I'll wear big old Jackie O. sunglasses and stowaway in first-class. The Senator won't even notice me. . . .

> HARRY
> I'm flying over there with Paige Katz.

Grace reacts—Harry immediately tries to mollify her.

> HARRY
> She speaks fluent Japanese, Grace. She has personal relationships with the people I'm supposed to meet—

> GRACE
> (recovering)
> It's okay.
> (smiles at Harry, emptily)
> It's fine.

> COTY (O.S.)
> Daddy, it's on!

LIVING ROOM— NIGHT

They arrange themselves before the altar of the television: Josie rocks Deirdre in her arms while Coty runs around the room like a dervish. Harry and Grace enter.

(CONTINUED)

> COTY
> It's eight o'clock! It's eight o'clock! It's eight o'clock!

> GRACE
> (to Harry)
> Did you check the box?

> HARRY
> (fiddling with box atop TV)
> It should work. . . .

> JOSIE
> 'Should'? That's all we need.

> HARRY
> It'll be fine. Bunch of worriers. . . .

> COTY
> (points to screen)
> There it is!

MUSIC. ON SCREEN GRAPHICS: "A SPECIAL PRESENTATION BY THE WILD PALMS NETWORK," followed by the jazzy WPN logo. Coty squeals with anticipation.

> GRACE
> Turn it up!

> JOSIE
> The adaptor's on?

> HARRY
> It's on, it's on!

> COTY
> Quiet!

Suddenly, a group of actors is dropped down into the Wyckoff living room: the HOLOSYNTH Coty, Tabba—and a REALTOR, who's "showing" them their new home. Deirdre goes over to Coty's HOLOSYNTH, mesmerized. Coty darts about, playfully "shadowing" his HOLOSYNTH, mimicking dialogue and movements; Harry has to restrain him.

> TABBA'S CHARACTER
> (looks around room)
> Hmmm. Not bad. Needs a little fixing up. . . .

> COTY'S CHARACTER
> (protesting)
> But, Ma—

(CONTINUED)

REALTOR'S CHARACTER
We handle all kinds of unusual properties. Moved
a young couple into an old mortuary last
week—very chic.

COTY'S CHARACTER
To die for.

LAUGHTRACK.

REALTOR'S CHARACTER
When did you say you lost your husband?

COTY'S CHARACTER
(sotto; contemptuous)
Nice segue.

LAUGHTRACK.

TABBA'S CHARACTER
A year ago. The strange thing is, he was a
minister. . . .

INT. WILD PALMS—NIGHT

Paige and the Senator are watching.

REALTOR'S CHARACTER
Then it's perfect. And the price is right. It's close
to the schools—and to God: He's a local call.

TABBA'S CHARACTER
Not everyone can say they have the Almighty as a
landlord.

COTY'S CHARACTER
Emphasis on Lord.

LAUGHTRACK. We PUSH IN ON the face of the Senator.

SENATOR
Now we have begun.

FADE OUT.

END OF ACT TWO

ACT THREE

FADE IN:

INT. HOUSE IN KYOTO—DAY

SUPERIMPOSE: "KYOTO, JAPAN," over traditional Japanese interior. Paige and Harry are in bed, in kimonos. Paige is flipping through a big book of prints and woodcuts.

                    HARRY
          It's funny—I feel like I've been here before.

                    PAIGE
          You're merely having a déjà vu from your samurai
          former life.

                    HARRY
          You do bring out the Toshira Mifune in me. All
          those Kurosawa films I saw when I was a kid—the
          warriors always fell in love with beautiful women
          who turned out to be ghosts.

She kisses him, then shows him some woodcuts in the book.

                    PAIGE
          Gorgeous, aren't they?

                    HARRY
          Hmmm. What's it called, again?

                    PAIGE
          'Ukiyo-e.'

                    HARRY
          Sounds like seafood.

                    PAIGE
          It means 'pictures from the floating world.'

                    HARRY
          Floating-world pictures—the critics used that for
          "Church Windows."

                    PAIGE
          Well, this is where they got it from.
                    (jumps up, exits frame)
          I have something for you. . . .

                    HARRY
          I hate it when you get up. This better be good.

She returns, holding two cups and a bottle of sake—a coiled snake is pickled in the latter.

                                        (CONTINUED)

HARRY
What the hell is that?

PAIGE
'Hebisake'—

HARRY
What do you do with it?

PAIGE
(pouring cups)
You drink it—

HARRY
You drink it. . . .

PAIGE
It's supposed to be an incredible aphrodisiac.

As they drink, they kiss.

PAIGE
This reminds me of something . . .

HARRY
I'm not even going to touch that.

PAIGE
There's a story they tell in Kyoto, from a
legend . . .

HARRY
Ukiyo-e.

PAIGE
A girl coming out of the water. It's haunting—

HARRY
That can be frightening, depending on weight.

PAIGE
(laughs)
Would you stop? This girl fell in love with a priest
who visited her village.

HARRY
Gimme that old-time religion.

PAIGE
When she told him how she felt, he said it was
impossible. She wouldn't listen, so he ran away to
the monastery.

HARRY
That wasn't very Zen.

(CONTINUED)

> PAIGE
> The girl followed, but came to a flooded river. She
> turned into a serpent and swam to the other side.
> The priest tried to hide under the temple's bronze
> bell—she found him there, and coiled around it.
> Her passion was so intense, the bell melted,
> killing them both.

He embraces her, bringing her down to the pillows.

EXT. HOUSE IN KYOTO—DAY

HIRO KOBASHI peers in furtively at the couple, then exits.

INT. KYOTO CLUB—NIGHT

Harry and Paige enter a small club—booths and a tiny stage. A
fiftyish hostess greets them. Paige speaks in Japanese, hands hostess a
cassette; the woman exits while they wait.

> PAIGE
> Ushio's wild about the Sixties. I got Chap to make
> a tape at the lab.

> HARRY
> Should have brought my Beatles boots. So you've
> met him before—this mysterious Ushio. . . .

Suddenly, CHAP STARFALL appears on b.g. stage—in Holosynth. He
sings The Beach Boys' "In My Room."

> CHAP
> 'There's a world where I can go and tell my
> secrets to . . . in my room—'

The hostess returns and leads them to booth. Three await them:
USHIO, around seventy, wispy beard, permanently gleeful;
HIDESATO, forties, buttoned-down businessman type; JITSUKO, a
dangerously pretty girl, twenty-ish. All stand, bow. (In following,
subtitled Japanese dialogue is indicated by underlining)

> USHIO
> Brian Wilson! Terrific! Thank you!

> PAIGE
> An honor to finally meet you.

> HIDESATO
> (re: Harry)
> He was to come alone.

> JITSUKO
> What crap!

                                                          (CONTINUED)

USHIO
(re: Paige)
Who is she?

HIDESATO
Paige Katz.

USHIO
Oh, terrific! I knew it!
(sniffs)
I smelled the lotion; Paige Katz uses too much
'Oiseaux.'

HIDESATO
(to Ushio)
What should we do?

USHIO
So much 'Oiseaux,' Ms. Katz! Lovely, but
overpowering.

PAIGE
(smiles)
Next time, I'll dilute it.

USHIO
I smell it on Harry Wyckoff!

HIDESATO
(polite)
Are you enjoying Kyoto, Mr. Wyckoff?

HARRY
It's lovely—though I haven't seen much of it. I
love the wood.

USHIO
Kyoto is a city of wood: cypress, ume,
sakura—but we have no palms! Do you miss the
wild palms?

HARRY
(smiles)
Not really.

USHIO
(to Hidesate; gleeful)
Make him talk some more!

JITSUKO
(friendly)
Will you have time to see the Golden Pavilion?

(CONTINUED)

                            HARRY
                    (as Ushio giggles)
I'd like that, but I'm afraid it's going to be a short
trip. My wife was pretty upset she couldn't come.

                            USHIO
Grace has every reason to be upset—she is losing
her mind!

                            HARRY
                        (to Paige)
What are they saying?

                            PAIGE
That . . . the Senator made a good choice in
having you represent him.

                            USHIO
Yes! Terrific choice! And how is Chickie Levitt?

                            HARRY
Chickie Levitt?

                        HIDESATO
Yes. How is he?

                            HARRY
                (looks at Paige; confused)
He's well.

                            USHIO
                        (delighted)
He doesn't know!

                            PAIGE
Harry visited Chickie just before we left.

                            HARRY
                (awkwardly improvising)
He's a little fragile, but seems happy.

                            USHIO
                        (gleeful)
Harry Wyckoff hasn't seen him! How
extraordinary!

                            PAIGE
Chickie's been ill.

                        JITSUKO
You murderous whore!

                            PAIGE
                        (to Jitsuko)
Enough!

                                    (CONTINUED)

> USHIO
> (to Jitsuko, stern)
> Respect!
> (to Paige; gleeful)
> Betrayed again! What a delight! What do they
> take me for, Miss Katz? An umbrella-maker?

> PAIGE
> <u>Chickie Levitt is well—you have my word.</u>

Jitsuko laughs.

> HIDESATO
> Sorry—we're through with you.

> JITSUKO
> Nothing for you here, Ms. Katz.

> PAIGE
> You promised us! The Senator—

> USHIO
> (delighted)
> <u>What arrogance! Just like Josie!</u> A message to the
> Senator, Ms. Katz: Tell the Master of Go that we
> have surrounded his 'stone.' Good-bye, Mr. Chip!

Ushio stands to exit.

> PAIGE
> Please—wait . . .

> USHIO
> 'In My Room'—that's where I belong. The Beach
> Boys sure got it right!

They exit.

> HARRY
> What's going on?

> PAIGE
> Someone's playing a game. We'll go back in the
> morning—

> HARRY
> Why were they asking me about Chickie?

> PAIGE
> Chickie works for us.
> HARRY
> He <u>what</u>?

> PAIGE
> I only found out two days ago myself—

(CONTINUED)

> HARRY
> You're lying!

> PAIGE
> That old man's got Chickie in an emotional
> stranglehold; he's holding onto Webware patents
> <u>Chickie</u> developed—do you know how much
> money we're talking about? <u>Hundreds of billions.</u>
> He's blackmailing us. . . .

> HARRY
> I don't like being ambushed, Paige. I don't know
> what I'm doing here, anyway. . . . Grace is barely
> out of the hospital—

Harry stands to exit.

> PAIGE
> You're here because you wanted to be with me.

> HARRY
> This doesn't feel right, Paige. I just want to get
> back to L.A.

Harry is exiting.

> PAIGE
> Wait for me . . .

> HARRY
> That's okay. The geisha's going for a walk . . .

> PAIGE
> (follows)
> They might follow you—they're dangerous.

> HARRY
> <u>Who's</u> dangerous, Paige? Tell me—I want to
> know. <u>Who's</u> dangerous?

As HIRO watches, Harry exits; Paige is helpless, turns reflexively.
Chap Starfall's begun a new song:

> CHAP
> <u>. . . and love will steer the stars! This is the</u>
> <u>dawning of the Age of Aquarius! Age of . . .</u>'

EXT. KYOTO BACK ALLEY—NIGHT

Harry walks along streets lit by ghostly lanterns bobbing in the soft
wind. Suddenly there is a voice.

> HIRO (O.S.)
> Harry Wyckoff!

(CONTINUED)

We PAN to reveal Hiro Kobashi.

                    HARRY
          Who are you?

                    HIRO
          A friend of Grace's. Please—off the streets!

INT. TEMPLE—NIGHT

They enter. The temple is dark, save for candles. Throughout scene,
Harry struggles to digest the onslaught of strange new information.

                    HIRO
          I watched you at the club.

                    HARRY
          How do you know my wife?

                    HIRO
          Grade school—a first love.

                    HARRY
          Why did you follow me?

                    HIRO
          Those people—they worked for Josie Ito's
          husband. The one she murdered.

                    HARRY
          Murdered—

                    HIRO
          His company was a rival of MimeCom. Kreutzer
          wanted to merge, but Ito wouldn't deal. He was
          found with a sword through the roof of his mouth;
          Josie invented a scandal, to explain the 'suicide.'

                    HARRY
                    (musing)
          Josie and Kreutzer . . . And what about Chickie
          Levitt?

                    HIRO
          MimeCom's bleeding his secrets. You were sent
          for the most coveted: a nanochip called 'GO.'

                    HARRY
          And the laughing old man?

                    HIRO
          Ushio Kawabata, Chickie's mentor. You met him
          once.

                                        (CONTINUED)

                         HARRY
No—I would have remembered.

                          HIRO
Under a different name: Terra.

                         HARRY
                      (incredulous)
The ballerina!

                          HIRO
In the Web, people look any way they want. . . .

A gleeful Ushio and his troupe—a few more now—enter. He claps
his hands together:

                         USHIO
Oh, this is too marvelous!

                         HARRY
What's happening?

                          HIRO
They're Friends, Harry . . .

                         USHIO
We have something for you.

                       HIDESATO
Couldn't give it before—

                         HARRY
Get your ass away from me!

                         USHIO
Too much Oiseaux—overpowering.

                        JITSUKO
Hold him!

                         HARRY
                      (outmuscled)
Help! Someone help me!

                       HIDESATO
              (rummaging into doctor's bag)
Here we go: 'hide and reveal.'

                          HIRO
They don't want Chickie hurt.

                         HARRY
                    (trying to assuage)
I think I know where he is—I'll make sure
Chickie's alright!

                                          (CONTINUED)

USHIO
Yes! Make sure, Harry!

HARRY
I only met him once, dammit!

JITSUKO
(sings softly)
<u>'In this world, I lock out all my worries and my
fears . . .'</u>

HARRY
Let me go and I'll help you!

Hidesato wields a scary-looking metal device; Harry eyes it with
horror.

USHIO
'Let me go.' Everybody wants to <u>go</u>—especially
Senator Kreutzer. He is the Go-Master. . . . And
Josie's the go-go girl!

HARRY
What are you going to do?

Jitsuko swabs one of Harry's hands with alcohol. Underlined
passages denote Japanese.

HIRO
Don't fight them!

JITSUKO
(singing)
'Now it's dark and I'm alone . . .'

USHIO
(singing)
<u>'In my room.'</u>
(to Harry)
The whole world's a tiny little room now, don't
you think, Harry?

Hidesato has his menacing device again; Harry eyes it, terrified.

HARRY
No!

JITSUKO
(singing)
'But I won't be afraid'—

USHIO
Everything must Go!

(CONTINUED)

                              HARRY
          Oh, God!

                    USHIO AND JITSUKO
                         (singing)
          'In my room . . .'

Ushio giggles weirdly as they bear down on Harry with his
"instrument," isolating a swabbed hand. Hidesato brings the machine
down . . .

EXT. GATE OF BUDDHIST TEMPLE—NIGHT

The WIND JOSTLES LANTERNS on empty streets. HARRY
SCREAMS.

                                              FADE OUT.

                    END OF ACT THREE

<u>ACT FOUR</u>

FADE IN:

INT. WYCKOFF HOUSE—ENTRANCE/LIVING ROOM—DAY

Grace answers the door in her robe—it's Gavin Whitehope's widow, EILEEN. She's very drunk. Her son, the Cop, watches anxiously from driveway; he's in uniform.

> EILEEN
>
> Hi there.

> GRACE
>
> Eileen—

> EILEEN
>
> Sorry about dropping in like this. That's my son—he didn't want me to come. He's embarrassed. . . . I've been drinking.

> GRACE
> (warm)
>
> Come in.

> EILEEN
> (staying put)
> That's okay. . . . You know, our little one's just five; he doesn't know what happened to his daddy.

> GRACE
>
> I'm so sorry, Eileen.

> EILEEN
>
> The police showed me pictures—of Gavin. I don't know why they did that. . . .

> GRACE
>
> The papers said it was political; that it was the Friends—

> EILEEN
>
> A <u>lie</u>! It was the Fathers! Damn them, Grace, damn them to Hell! I'm not supposed to say that, but what difference does it make—now?
> (ironic)
> Not going to turn me in to Channel Three, are ya, Grace? Hey: I almost forgot. I brought you something.

She takes a little black rhino from her pocket and hands it to Grace, who seems to recognize it.

(CONTINUED)

> GRACE
> Where did you get this?

> EILEEN
> Gavin had it in his pocket when they found him. I
> thought it belonged to one of the kids, then I
> remembered: The night we had dinner, Coty
> showed his collection of sweet rhinoceri.
> Grace . . . why would Gavin steal something from
> a child?

She stands, goes to door.

> EILEEN
> You know, Timmy—he's our youngest—Timmy
> sings a song Gavin taught him: 'What IS that
> climbing up my stair? It's not a boar, it's not a
> bear! And on its snout it has a horn, as odd as any
> unicorn'—

Grace opens the door for her. Eileen's son exits car, walks to f.g.
Grace watches the son rush to his mother, catching her before she
tipsily falls. Eileen turns back to Grace.

> EILEEN
> 'But wait! There must be three or four who've
> wobbled through my kitchen door. And though it
> seems preposterous . . .'

Grace closes door, examines the disturbing plastic creature.

INT. COTY'S ROOM—DAY

Grace enters. Coty is staring at her; we get the sense she was
expected.

> GRACE
> What happened to Gavin Whitehope?

> COTY
> Are you drunk?

> GRACE
> Did you hurt Gavin? Talk to me!

> COTY
> Get off a me!

> GRACE
> Was Grammie with you? Did she make you? Did
> Grammie make you, Coty? Baby, answer me!

> COTY
> (half-tearful, half-defiant)
> I did it myself!

(CONTINUED)

> GRACE
> (unhinged)
> Oh God! What am I going to do? You're still my
> baby . . .

> COTY
> Let me go!

She releases him; he runs from the room.

> GRACE
> (shattered; to self)
> You're just a boy . . . I won't let them hurt you—

INT. THERAPIST'S OFFICE—DAY

Harry on the couch, unburdening himself to Dr. Schenkl. He traces
his thumb over the small, dirty bandage that covers the wound
between thumb and forefinger.

> HARRY
> I thought they were going to kill me—a crazy
> voice kept going through my head, over and over:
> 'I'm going to die in a temple in Kyoto.'

> TOBIAS
> (re: wound)
> Have you seen a doctor?

> HARRY
> (shakes head)
> I still don't know how I got back from the temple.
> Paige found me the next morning, outside the
> house. It was drizzling—the perfect picture of a
> floating world. An hour later we were in the air,
> on our way back to L.A. The city looked like a
> parody—David Hockney's Guernica. Still, I was
> glad to be home. I didn't feel like a samurai
> anymore . . .
> (laughs)
> . . . or a geisha.

INT. WYCKOFF HOUSE—ENTRANCE—NIGHT

Harry home from work; TAMBOR anxiously approaches, talks in
hushed tones.

> TAMBOR
> Harry—it's Grace!

> HARRY
> What is it?

(CONTINUED)

                              TAMBOR
            She's been upstairs for hours, watching holotapes
            of Coty—there's something <u>creepy</u> . . .

Harry hurriedly exits upstairs.

MASTER BEDROOM

Harry enters the darkened room. Coty's holosynth moves in eerie
SLOW MOTION—like a drugged ghost.

Grace is in bed, passed out. On the bed, atop her black jigsaw
puzzle, are dozens of unsent letters. He examines one—the envelope
is addressed to "Eli Levitt, STATE PERCEPTORY, INDIAN WELLS." He
opens it and retrieves the letter within, which begins: "Dearest Father,
Each time I begin a letter . . ."

EXT. RESORT—STATE PERCEPTORY—DAY

ESTABLISHING SHOT.

INT. RESORT—INFIRMARY—DAY

Harry is led down a row of beds by smiling NURSE, who exits. A
pale Eli Levitt lays in one of them, listening to portable radio.

                              HARRY
            Hello.

                               ELI
            I like listening to the radio—<u>safer</u> than the damn
            television.

                              HARRY
                            (smiles)
            I know what you mean.

                               ELI
            Visitors aren't usually allowed here—guess you
            got <u>juice.</u>

                              HARRY
            You have a flu?

                               ELI
            A small case of mood poisoning; must be
            something I hate.

                              HARRY
            I'm not sure exactly why I came here.

                               ELI
            Join the club.

> HARRY
> (beat)
> I know who you are.

> ELI
> Grace told you?

> HARRY
> No. I had my suspicions.

> ELI
> The world would be a terrible place without them.

> HARRY
> For a while, I thought you were an old lover.

Eli laughs.

> HARRY
> Why was it a secret all these years?

> ELI
> Shame, embarrassment—her mama did a pretty
> good number on her. The Friends have a
> nickname for Josie: 'Hannya'—female demon.
> Why that woman's let me live all these years, I'll
> never know. Sexual obsession, I imagine.

> HARRY
> A friend of mine was arrested . . .

> ELI
> Tommy Laszlo.

Harry is surprised; Eli laughs, muses.

> ELI
> There was a famous chemist, back in the Sixties.
> He was playing around with the <u>fugu</u>—puffer fish.
> Ever heard of it? A delicacy in Japan. The dose in
> a single fish can kill; a lesser amount gets you
> high. MimeCom grabbed it, tweaked it, and came
> up with something of their own—they call it
> Mimezine.

> HARRY
> What does this have to do with Tommy?

> ELI
> Better images through chemistry—smashing the
> reality barrier. It allows you to interact with
> holograms. Is it real or is it
> MimeCom?—impossible to tell.

(CONTINUED)

                    HARRY
Go on.

                     ELI
Beware the mimetaur, Mr. Wyckoff! They want to
fold the whole thing into television—Tommy
knew that. Tommy knew a lot more . . .

                    HARRY
I don't understand—

                     ELI
'Church Windows' is <u>nothing</u>: the fingerbowl for
the entree.
                    (sings)
'Mi-me-zine grace, how sweet the sound, that
saved a wretch like me . . .'

                    HARRY
What does it do?

                     ELI
In large amounts? It nails you to the cross of your
own awareness—rather like being date-raped by
Nirvana. Quite a package for the masses; see, the
Senator needs energy for his 'final flight'—all that
business with the GO chip. He needs
support—like a king held aloft by the minds of his
minions. He is our Alexander—he'll conquer the
countries of our imaginations, one by one, and we
will dream him into infinity.
                    (laughs)
That famous chemist I was talking about, the
pioneer who started it all? His name was Dex
Wyckoff—your daddy.

                    HARRY
                   (stunned)
You knew my father?

                     ELI
No. But the Senator did.
                    (beat)
They were partners.

EXT. POOL AT HIGH-RISE—DAY

Josie and a group of Japanese businessmen are having lunch by the
pool. The men are laughing at something she said, when Grace
approaches from b.g.—thoroughly bent out of shape.

                    GRACE
Mother?

                                        (CONTINUED)

> JOSIE
> Darling, what a surprise!
> (to men)
> This is my daughter, Grace—

> GRACE
> (shouts)
> What have you done to him?

> JOSIE
> (awkward)
> What are you talking about?

> GRACE
> He's killing for you now!

> JOSIE
> My daughter's been ill. Would you excuse us?

She takes Grace by the hand and leads her around corner.

CABANA

Once out of guests' sight, she viciously punches Grace in the gut—Grace doubles over, reeling into wall. Then she gut punches her again.

> JOSIE
> You've got a hell of a mouth on you: Watch someone doesn't take a needle and sew it up.

> GRACE
> You leave that little boy alone!

> JOSIE
> Don't insult me by pretending you don't know what's happening! You knew from the beginning—weak dog! Listen to me: We have come too far to be terrorized by your prim sensitivities—do I make myself clear?
> (slaps her again)
> Answer me!

> GRACE
> Yes!

EXT. STREETS—DAY

Grace drives, holding hand to cheek—bloodied and crying.
Suddenly, Peter rises up from the back seat, where he's been hiding.
Grace is startled.

> GRACE
> What are you doing!

(CONTINUED)

                              PETER
          It's Peter.

She pulls over.

                              GRACE
          How did you get in the car—

                              PETER
          Hiro's coming.

                              GRACE
          Hiro? When?

                              PETER
          Soon.

                              GRACE
          Who are you?

He unbuttons his shirt, revealing tattoos. Mesmerized, she reaches out to touch them with her fingertips.

                              GRACE
          What . . . are they—

                              PETER
          They're pictures. Pictures of the floating world.

INT. METROPOLITAN DETENTION CENTER—NIGHT

A nightwatch GUARD walks past cells, peering into each. He pauses at Tommy's. The TV's ON—Tommy sits on the edge of his bed, watching.

                              GUARD
          What are you watching there?

No answer.

                              GUARD
          Laszlo?

No answer.

                              GUARD
          Laszlo! Answer me when I talk to you—

Tommy "flickers"—he's merely a projected image. The Guard immediately unlocks cell door, enters. He stands before "Tommy," then turns to TV and lifts box sitting atop: It's a contraband, jerrybuilt Mimadaptor, held together with tape and screwdriver. Realizing what's happened, the Guard picks it up and hurls it against the wall—the holosynth of Tommy vanishes with the Mimadaptor's destruction.

                                              (CONTINUED)

EXT. WILD PALMS—GUEST HOUSE—NIGHT

Establishing shot.

INT. WILD PALMS—GUEST HOUSE—NIGHT

Chickie sweats in his wheelchair, while Chap directs a light on his "subject."

                    CHICKIE
          Terra doesn't know anything!

                    CHAP
          She's more than just an innocent 'ballerina. . . .'
          That old man in Kyoto shouldn't have betrayed
          you, Chickie—you could've been back at the
          beach by now.

                    CHICKIE
          Ushio didn't betray me!

                    CHAP
          Ushio is the ballerina, can't you see that? Ushio is
          Terra—

                    CHICKIE
          Liar!

                    CHAP
          Talk to me, Chickie! Tell me about the GO chip
          or Terra's gonna hurt, it's that simple. She's
          already in pain; don't make it worse. Tell me your
          secrets. Help the Senator, and Terra will be free.

CAMERA PANS TO EXTREME CLOSEUP of Chickie's "ei(detic)glasses" on the bedside table: We see the computer-generated Terra in one of the lenses, her mouth open in a silent scream.

INT. WYCKOFF HOUSE—BATHROOM—NIGHT

Harry enters, removing towel. He steps into the steamy shower.

HALLWAY

Grace makes way to Coty's room. She hears Coty's voice; stops outside Deirdre's door. Coty is singing softly to his sister:

                    COTY
          "What IS that climbing up my stair? It's not a boar,
          it's not a bear! And on its snout it has a horn, as
          odd as any unicorn—"

Grace looks down at her hand as she opens it: The tiny plastic rhino is held within.

                                        (CONTINUED)

BATHROOM

Harry holds the hand with the dirty Band-Aid out from the spray of water; it's been there since the temple incident in Kyoto. He slowly peels it back—a look of horror.

HALLWAY

Grace lingers at door as Coty continues to read.

> HARRY (O.S.)
> Grace? Grace!

She runs back toward room. They meet in hallway—Harry, in towel, dripping wet.

> GRACE
> What is it?

Harry holds his hand out for her to see—it is the tattoo of the Wild Palms. Coty comes out, holding Deirdre by hand.

> GRACE
> (stares at tattoo)
> No!

> HARRY
> (panicky)
> Grace, what is it?

> GRACE
> (screams)
> No! No! No-o-o-o-o-o!

> FADE OUT.

THE END

WILD PALMS

Fourth Hour

"Rising Sons"

ACT ONE

FADE IN:

EXT. WILD PALMS—BACK YARD—DAY

The SENATOR sits on back terrace playing GO with Asian
manservant. Only a few feet away, three girls in gaudy makeup and
short skirts—a Japanese version of The Supremes—loudly sing:

> GIRL GROUP
> 'Love child! Never meant to be . . . Love child!
> Born in poverty—'

> HARRY
> (enters from house)
Hello!

> SENATOR
> (to Harry)
Hold on!
> (to self)
Now where the hell'd I leave that?

He finds remote control, TURNS DOWN SOUND—it's a holosynth.
The girls remain throughout scene, doing their routine, MOS. The
manservant bows, exits.

> SENATOR
Well, well, the Illustrated Man! Let's have a look!
> (examines Harry's tattoo)
A beauty!

> HARRY
What's it all about?

> SENATOR
Ushio—your tattoo artist—took something from
us. We offered him money for the stolen goods,
and it wasn't enough; he marked you because he
knew I'd be annoyed. And I am. But don't you
worry, Harry. All is well!

> HARRY
I saw Eli Levitt last week.

> SENATOR
There's a name I Haven't heard in a while.

(CONTINUED)

                    HARRY
He said you knew my father.

                    SENATOR
That I did.
                    (nods at board)
Your dad was the one who taught me how to play
GO. Dex was the real thing—the Chickie of his
day.

                    HARRY
How did you meet?

                    SENATOR
At a commune near Sebastopol—where you were
born. Ol' Dex was legendary for two things: the
purity of his L.S.D., and the fact he was never
seen without a necktie.

Laughs.

                    HARRY
And my mother?

                    SENATOR
A hippie girl! In those days, what we
affectionately called a freak.

                    HARRY
What was her name?

                    SENATOR
Bernice—like the constellation, Coma Berenices.
Hated that name. Called herself 'Marrakech' for
awhile—that was the Sixties.

                    HARRY
What did she look like?

                    SENATOR
Joni Mitchell. You don't know Joni Mitchell, do
you?

The Senator changes TV channel; suddenly, in place of the singers,
there is a black-and-white Frankenstein monster, kneeling with a little
girl (also black-and-white).

                    SENATOR
Your father wanted to use computers to free the
brain from the body. This was back in the '70s;
there wasn't even video! Critics dismissed him as
an acid casualty—which he was! The scientific
community thought of him as nothing more than a
performance artist.

                                        (CONTINUED)

> HARRY
> What happened?

> SENATOR
> Blew his face off with a shotgun. Because of
> recoil, the coroner said the first shot wasn't
> fatal—ten minutes later, Dex finished the job. I've
> often wondered what went through his mind those
> last ten minutes.

EXT. MELROSE AVENUE—DAY

An UNKEMPT GIRL stands on sidewalk in the middle of an
evangelist-style rant.

> UNKEMPT GIRL
> (rapid)
> 'Church Windows'? Whose Church? The Church
> of MimeCom and the New Realists? Connect the
> dots, people! In Senator Kreutzer's Constitution,
> Church and State are one—

GRACE WYCKOFF ENTERS FRAME, is handed a flyer as she passes.
HIRO KOBASHI ENTERS FRAME, tapping Grace's shoulder as she
walks, still reading flyer.

> HIRO
> Miss? Can you tell me the time?

> GRACE
> (looks at watch, then looks up)
> Hiro!

They embrace.

INT. "EROS + MASSACRE" COFFEEHOUSE—DAY

The excited old friends have cappuccino in a booth of the bohemian,
book-lined cafe.

> GRACE
> You look exactly the same—so handsome . . .

> HIRO
> Remember the Star Trek thing we did? You know,
> Spock and Kirk at the S&M bar—

> TOGETHER
> Beat me up, Scotty!

They laugh.

(CONTINUED)

> GRACE
>
> I've missed you so much! I don't know why I never wrote. When Josie moved us to the States, it was like starting over—I didn't want to look back.

> HIRO
>
> It doesn't matter, Grace . . .

> GRACE
>
> It's like I dreamed Japan, and everyone in it. How's your father?

> HIRO
>
> He died, four years ago—in Tokyo's version of the Resort.

> GRACE
> (touches hand, consoling)
>
> Hiro . . .

> HIRO
> (mordant)
>
> We call 'em 'satoriums.' Our best people seem to vanish into thin air.
> (outraged)
> They're in the temples now—Synthiotics, in the temples!

> GRACE
>
> I'm caught, Hiro! It's like they've stung me and I can't move!
> (shows her wrist scar)
> See my 'bracelet'?

> HIRO
> (moved)
>
> There is a way out, Grace. You've got friends—

> GRACE
> (shakes her head)
>
> Too late . . .

> HIRO
>
> You've got to talk to Harry—you know the danger he's in. You're the only one he'll listen to . . .

> GRACE
>
> They've got their hooks in him—you don't know what it's been like. Paige Katz—all of them . . .

> HIRO
>
> Try! Pull yourself together—if he doesn't listen, then you run . . .

(CONTINUED)

GRACE
To where, Hiro? Where are we all going to run to?
Paradise?

EXT. LITTLE TOKYO BATHHOUSE—DAY

A WAGON BRAKES HARD in front of a traditional <u>sento</u>, where
attendants await at entrance. Stitch and his men form a shield around
Tommy as they hustle him inside.

INT. LITTLE TOKYO BATHHOUSE—DAY

Tommy is moved into bathing area—the pool is emptied of water.
They walk him into empty basin, where TULLY WOIWODE and
aides await. The pool is "furnished" with tables and chairs. Tully
Woiwode and Tommy embrace. Tommy is out of it.

WOIWODE
How's my Houdini?

STITCH
He's a little shaky.

WOIWODE
(to Tommy)
Some escape you pulled—Chickie taught you
good stuff, huh?

STITCH
We found him in the L.A. River.

WOIWODE
(to Tommy)
At least you picked a dry place.

TOMMY
My head hurts—they gave me something in
jail . . .

STITCH
(to Woiwode)
Mimezine.

TOMMY
I'm okay. Only thing is I—I seem to see . . .
cathedrals.

WOIWODE
Cathedrals?

TOMMY
That's the main side effect of the drug—so far. I
mean, I <u>really see them.</u>

(CONTINUED)

                              STITCH
Next time you do, just look. Don't go inside to
pray. Okay?

All laugh.

                              TOMMY
Sorry about your eyes, Tully.

                              WOIWODE
I got you back—that's all that counts.

INT./EXT. SKELETAL BEACH HOUSE—DAY

Harry walks Grace through an empty house.

                              HARRY
Don't you think it's weird that the Senator knew
my parents? The guy told me more in 30 minutes
than I found out in <u>four years</u> of headshrinking.

                              GRACE
You should get a refund. Harry, what are we
doing here? I need to get back to the store.

                              HARRY
                        (surveys house)
What do you think?

                              GRACE
About what?

                              HARRY
The Senator gave me a chunk of stock—options
vested over ten years.
                        (looks around)
So I bought it.

                              GRACE
You <u>bought</u> this? Oh, Harry—

                              HARRY
Two million.
          (sings, dances à la James Brown)
'<u>I feel good! Like I knew that I would now</u>'—
                   (as she starts to cry)
What's wrong?

                              GRACE
They're buying you—

                              HARRY
                        (irate)
What?

                                                    (CONTINUED)

GRACE
Can't you see what's happening?

HARRY
Wait a minute.
(beat)
You wanted this too, remember?

GRACE
No, Harry—not this! It's a sham! You don't know
how dangerous that man is!

HARRY
(sarcastic)
Here we go: Senator Tony Kreutzer, big bad bully
of the Brave New World. A hard rain's gonna fall,
right, Grace? Well, let it!

GRACE
I don't know you anymore.

HARRY
That makes two of us. Why didn't you tell me Eli
Levitt was your father?

GRACE
I . . . I couldn't—

HARRY
Sort of strange, isn't it? Married twelve years and
you lie about something like that! What else are
you lying about?

GRACE
I didn't want to bring you into it—I thought they'd
leave us alone . . .

HARRY
(almost mocking)
'They'? 'They' who, the Mafia? Did I marry into
the Mob, Grace? I mean, who am I supposed to
believe? You sit there with your nineteen nervous
breakdowns—

GRACE
Goddam you! That technology he's developed is
addictive—

HARRY
Yeah, yeah, they said that about TV fifty years
ago—and they were wrong.

GRACE
We're not talking Thomas Edison here! One day,
(MORE)

(CONTINUED)

                    GRACE (CONT'D)
in the middle of 'Church Windows,' we'll find our
country no longer belongs to us—and no one'll
even care! Wild Palms <u>silences</u> their enemies,
Harry: with artificial dreams—and real death
squads!

                    HARRY
The 'conspiracy from Hell.' You know what? Life
is a conspiracy, against all of us: You either run
for the hills with your tail between your legs—or
stick around and fight for the beach house!

                    GRACE
Spoken like a true New Realist.

                    HARRY
And what's wrong with that?

                    GRACE
                (laughs weirdly)
For one thing, your 'son' is a murderer—and you
stand here giving media lectures!

                    HARRY
                (humoring her)
My son's a murderer? Who'd he kill, Grace?
Rocky and Bullwinkle?

                    GRACE
Gavin Whitehope.

                    HARRY
                (worried about her)
Maybe you should think about going back to the
hospital.

                    GRACE
How about the Resort? I'd be closer to
Daddy—and you'd have lots of free time to spend
with your <u>girlfriend!</u>

                    HARRY
                (a beat)
We stopped all that, after Japan.

                    GRACE
It doesn't matter anymore. Please, Harry—I want
to go home.

INT. WILD PALMS—GUEST HOUSE—NIGHT

(CONTINUED)

A uniformed figure surreptitiously enters. CLOSE ON name tag: WHITEHOPE JR. PULL BACK to reveal Gavin Whitehope's son, who we saw earlier, when his mother visited Grace to return Coty's stolen rhino. Chickie's in his bed, typing on computer console; the computer sits on a tray that swivels over his lap.

> GAVIN JR.
> Mr. Levitt?
> (as Chickie looks up)
> They killed my father—I want to help.

He hands him a small white sack.

> GAVIN JR.
> Chocolate cookies—tell them Josie gave them to you. They're laced with Mimezine.

Suddenly, CHAP STARFALL enters, holding a golf club.

> CHAP
> (to guard)
> What's going on?

> GAVIN JR.
> I heard a scream . . .

> CHICKIE
> I fell asleep—had a nightmare.

> CHAP
> (to guard)
> You can go.

Gavin Jr. exits.

> CHICKIE
> How was the game?

> STARFALL
> Think I need a new handicap.

> CHICKIE
> I feel the same way.

> STARFALL
> What's in the bag?

> CHICKIE
> Cookies—Josie brought them.

> STARFALL
> Cookies from Josie? That's enough to make anybody scream.
> (reaches inside; takes a nibble of one)
> (MORE)

(CONTINUED)

STARFALL (CONT'D)
You oughta cut down on the sugar.
(finishes cookie)
It's the only vice I have left.

CHICKIE
When will they let me go, Chap?

STARFALL
Soon as you give him the GO chip.

CHICKIE
It doesn't exist, Chap—it's a fiction . . .

STARFALL
Just like Terra, huh?

CHICKIE
Terra's real—

STARFALL
Maybe she's like a song—I mean, where does a
song go, when you're not singing it?
(starts to exit)
There's one for the philosophers.

CHICKIE
Wait! I made something for you, with the
keyboard. A custom program . . .

STARFALL
Not tonight, I have a headache.

CHICKIE
Please, Chap? I worked hard on it.

Chickie hands him pair of "eiglasses." Starfall sits on bed with a sigh.

STARFALL
What we do for love. . . . I'm a good whore—go
where I'm kicked; you oughta do the same.
(puts on glasses)
This better be good, puppy dog.

We PUSH IN ON Chickie.

INT. NIGHTCLUB—NIGHT

Starfall, still in golf clothes, finds himself in dark, smoky room, lit in
such a way we can't see patrons' faces. A man onstage sits on a
stool, back to audience. APPLAUSE as he faces the crowd—he is
Starfall's exact double. Chap is amused.

(CONTINUED)

The Double counts "Uh-one, and uh-two, and—": an unseen BAND BEGINS. As the Double sings, he walks over to Starfall, who's enjoying the cleverness of Chickie's customized gift.

> DOUBLE
> 'I love the looks of you, the lure of you, the sweet of you and the pure of you—'

Starfall is abruptly grabbed by patrons. We see their "faces" for the first time—smooth and featureless, except for one: Terra, in ballerina attire.

> DOUBLE
> 'The eyes, the arms, and the mouth of you . . . the east, west, north—and the south of you!'

The Double's already reached him; as he sings, he thrusts his fist into Starfall's mouth. In a matter of seconds, with great, horrifying, wiggly force, the arm has weirdly—impossibly—disappeared down the singer's throat, right up to the Double's armpit. Audience APPLAUSE throughout.

> DOUBLE
> 'I'd love to gain complete control of you—and handle even the heart and soul of you! So love at least a small percent of me, do . . . 'cause I—love—all—of—you!'

The Double yanks arm out as Starfall drops to floor.

INT. WILD PALMS—GUEST HOUSE—DUSK

Chap lays on the bed, twitching—bleeding from the ears. Chickie cries softly, with remorse; tenderly removes Chap's eiglasses.

> CHICKIE
> I'm . . . sorry—never wanted to kill anyone! Why don't you just leave Terra alone, all of you? Leave her alone!

FADE OUT.

END OF ACT ONE

<u>ACT TWO</u>

FADE IN:

INT. WYCKOFF HOUSE—BACK YARD—MORNING

Grace sits on a chaise by the pool, drinking.

> GRACE
> (to self)
> Today is the first day of the rest of your wife . . .

She sees a figure coming toward her; stands.

> GRACE
> Hiro! What's happened?

> HIRO
> Your father escaped last night.

> GRACE
> Is he all right?

> HIRO
> (nods)
> It's an embarrassment to the Senator—he's
> orchestrated a news blackout.

> GRACE
> Can you take me to him?

Hiro nods.

EXT. BEL-AIR HOUSE—TERRACE/POOL/ZEN GARDEN

They overlook Zen garden, where there's a TV and standard box
atop. The Senator carries a very large holocassette. TABBA
SCHWARTKOPF sunbathes, listens to radio; turns on her stomach to
watch and listen.

> HARRY
> I keep thinking about Miss Alabama—that kiss . . .

> SENATOR
> Sex is <u>the</u> monster in the box—<u>major</u> research
> area, we just don't talk about it.

> TABBA
> Love among consenting holograms.

> SENATOR
> I have a little surprise for you. . . .
> (slips cassette into recorder)
> I found an old photo of your father.

(CONTINUED)

                              HARRY
You're kidding.

                              SENATOR
What you're about to see is a 3-D animated
rendering with texture mapping and full-motion
algorithms—

                              HARRY
                         (nervously jokey)
That's easy for <u>you</u> to say.

Suddenly, DEX WYCKOFF appears on the terrace. Harry goes into
shock as Tabba walks over, curious.

                              SENATOR
It's only a thirty-second program—not very
elaborate . . .

                              HARRY
This . . . is my father?

                              SENATOR
Looks more like Dex than Dex did.

"Dex Wyckoff" moves toward his son; his voice wavery:

                              DEX
Harry . . . ? Harry . . . ?

                              HARRY
                         (spooked; enthralled)
No!

                              SENATOR
The voice is a little hinky—we kluged it off some
gameshow host.

                              DEX
                         (to Harry)
<u>It is an honest ghost, that let me tell you.</u>

                              SENATOR
Hamlet: my idea.

                              TABBA
That's really in poor taste, Tony.

                              HARRY
                         (incredulous)
He's staring at me—

Dex extends his arms toward Harry, in a hug.

                                              (CONTINUED)

> SENATOR
> It ends with the hug—go ahead, Harry, don't be
> shy!

Harry raises arms slowly, as if on instinct alone.

> SENATOR
> That's right, Harry: storm the memory palace!

Just as the two are about to "embrace," Dex vanishes leaving Harry to
hug thin air. The program's over.

EXT. LITTLE TOKYO BATHHOUSE—DAY

ESTABLISHING SHOT.

INT. LITTLE TOKYO BATHHOUSE—FURNISHED POOL—DAY

A curtain is set up at the shallow-end deck. Down in the pool, Hiro
embraces Friends, speaks Japanese. CAMERA PANS TO Grace,
hugging her fugitive father in tearful reunion.

> ELI
> It's not safe here, Grace—

> GRACE
> There is no 'safe' anymore! You sent me away
> once—never again. I can't stay in their world
> anymore.

> ELI
> I know, baby. I know.

> GRACE
> They took my son; I know it now. I won't go
> back!

> TOMMY
> (pulls curtain open, enters)
> It's showtime!

Eli takes out handkerchief, dries her eyes; she smiles at his
ministrations. The lights dim and the curtain parts: All in pool turn
their attention to curtain as they draw open—MUSIC BEGINS. Men
and women drink wine and sake and eat from paper plates—a festive
celebration for the escapee. Throughout scene, INTERCUT
audience—Tommy, Grace, Eli, Hiro, et al.—laughing appreciatively.

Wearing heavy "tan" makeup, a running suit with Wild Palms logo
and a distinctive white toupee, Stitch Walken enters to applause and
derisive laughter. He begins jogging in place—and sings in a
grotesque impersonation of the Senator.

> STITCH/SENATOR
> <u>'Love laughs at a King, Kings don't mean a thing,</u>
> <u>on the street of dreams!'</u>
> (sees someone O.S.)
> Hiya, Josie!

The crowd goes wild as the blind Woiwode enters with the help of an aide, who sits him in a chair. Woiwode is in drag—kabuki makeup, sunglasses and wig, the bust heavily padded beneath one of Josie's signature dresses. His imitation of Josie's voice and mannerisms is dead-on.

> WOIWODE/JOSIE
> (distraught; fanning himself)
> How can you sing at a time like this?

> STITCH/SENATOR
> A time like what, Dragon Lady?

> WOIWODE/JOSIE
> (steamy)
> I <u>love</u> it when you call me that.

Laughter.

> WOIWODE/JOSIE
> (agitated)
> Tommy and Eli have escaped! I'm so scared!
> What are we gonna do?

> STITCH/SENATOR
> Calm down, Josie. Take a deep breath and repeat
> after me: 'Everything must go, everything must go,
> everything must—'

Laughter.

> WOIWODE/JOSIE
> (hot and bothered)
> I haven't been able to sleep since they busted Eli
> Levitt from the Resort.

> STITCH/SENATOR
> Worried he'll creep into your room in the middle
> of the night and do unspeakable things?

> WOIWODE/JOSIE
> (trembling with desire)
> You mean, like tie me up and pelt me with
> sashimi?

Laughter.

(CONTINUED)

> WOIWODE/JOSIE
> I know who's behind it all: Tully Woiwode! I'll
> have to keep my eyes on him. . . .

> STITCH/SENATOR
> Guess that's fair—his eyes were all over you.

Howls, laughter, AD LIBS of mock outrage from audience. Eli holds
Grace's hand—grateful to be together.

INT. WILD PALMS GUEST HOUSE—DAY

Chickie lays in bed; bound and gagged. JOSIE pours herself a drink
from a bottle of hebisake, the "snake-in-the-bottle."

> JOSIE
> That was a terrible thing you did.
> (beat)
> Chap was trying to help. Everyone's pulling for
> you and here you are, obstinate and
> murderous—dangling precariously over the fires
> we have lit in your mind. What a waste. You
> could be sharing so much.

She goes to mirror, preens.

> JOSIE
> I used to be gorgeous. Eli always said I looked like
> Julie Christie. Boy, did he have a thing for Julie
> Christie—probably had her.

She takes pair of "eiglasses" from table, walks them to Chickie.

> JOSIE
> Terra's going to suffer for your cruelties—oh, yes.
> They sent a virus after your fragile black
> paramour: It'll catch her, and eat her—just like a
> Grimm fairy tale! Here—take a look . . .

She puts the glasses on his face.

CLOSE ON LENS

Terra screaming, MOS.

We ENTER the lens: Terra runs for her life, pursued by something
bestial. [COMPUTER FX]. It swallows her up.

INT. WILD PALMS—SENATOR'S BEDROOM—DAY

The Senator screams, sits upright in bed. Paige enters. She mops his
brow. Curtains blow into room from open windows.

PAIGE
I'm here! It's all right.

SENATOR
Napping; had a nightmare.
(stands; goes to window)
Always the same. Daddy brings me to visit
her—Mother, at Manzanar. But nothing's there,
only dunes. He hands me a shovel. I'm only a
boy; it's hard to dig in the sand. He grabs it and
in seconds, he's dug a great pit. Orders me in; I
plead, but he just laughs. I climb into the pit . . .

PAIGE
Don't think about it anymore—

SENATOR
Am I ever going to leave this earth?

PAIGE
Yes—

SENATOR
Chickie Levitt's a crippled little liar! He's holding
out on me: a fiasco of red herrings. They're
alchemists, Paige! Ushio and his 47 Ronin! You
know what 'infinity' is for them? A cologne you
dab behind the ears! It's that easy—they know
what to do with the memories of old men.

PAIGE
Tony, you have a fever.

SENATOR
Don't humor me! They'll come after me now:
Tommy and that lord of the flies, Eli Levitt.
(to Paige)
Come closer!

She does.

SENATOR
They'll try to bury me in the sand.
(kisses her neck; she's not into it)
I'm going to put the tape on. Do you mind?

Paige says nothing. He slips a large cassette in the machine. A
dancing woman appears, in holosynth—she wears a tight dress and
moves sensually to accompanying TRACK, "Wedding Bell Blues." The
Senator keeps an eye on her, as if that's the thing that guarantees his
arousal. Paige barely conceals her disgust.

SENATOR
What's the matter?

(CONTINUED)

                          PAIGE
I'm tired, that's all.

                          SENATOR
                    (proffering eyedropper)
          A little Mimezine'll pick you up—

                          PAIGE
You're sick!

                          SENATOR
                    (smiles; foxy)
          It's Harry. You're in love with him, aren't you?

                          PAIGE
I'm not in love with anyone; I don't even know
what the word means. You fixed all that—happy?

She storms out. The dancing woman moves closer. The Senator
smiles to self, puts eyedropper to his tongue, then settles back on
sheets for the "show."

INT. MALIBU BEACH HOUSE—NIGHT

Paige answers the door; it's mellow Harry.

                          HARRY
Sorry to bother you. I was in a little pile-up down
the road: bodies everywhere. I was just wondering
if I could use the phone, freshen up, have a
drink—
                    (she's been crying)
Hey now, what's the matter?
                    (follows her in)
Is it about Tommy breaking out?

                          PAIGE
I'm just feeling sorry for myself, that's all.

                          HARRY
                    (droll)
That is such a turn-on. Mind if I join you?

                          PAIGE
What are you feeling sorry about?

                          HARRY
Marriage is in shambles. My wife thinks I've
become this off-the-wall cultist, seduced by
money and power.

                          PAIGE
Is she right?

                                        (CONTINUED)

                    HARRY
The thought's crossed my mind.

                    PAIGE
What else you feeling sorry about?

                    HARRY
Let's see. Never got to know Daddy . . . Hairline's
receding . . . No one likes my beach house—

                    PAIGE
                   (smiles)
Sorry to hear that.

                    HARRY
Your turn.

                    PAIGE
Aside from being scared all the time? I wake up at
night, and I can't breathe . . .

                    HARRY
Let's get outta here.

                    PAIGE
Where?

                    HARRY
Someplace we can have a few laughs—we could
use it.

INT. UNDERGROUND CLUB—NIGHT

Harry and Paige are let through tables of smoky room by hostess—a
mixture of the conservative and the bohemian.

                    HARRY
Think he's crazy?

                    PAIGE
A little.

                    HARRY
Know what he told me? That he was going to run
for President—that he wanted me in the Cabinet!

                    PAIGE
Just draw the line when he asks you to wear the
pink pillbox hat.

                    HARRY
He calls me in the middle of the night, says <u>weird</u>
stuff—talks about the GO chip and something
called the 'tama.'

(CONTINUED)

> PAIGE
> That means 'soul.'

> HARRY
> Whatever. Says he's harnessed the tama and
> locked it inside a household shrine: the television!

> VOICE (O.S.)
> You've seen him on 'Laugh Attack'—Ladies and
> gentlemen, put your hands together for the very
> strange, very bitter comedy stylings of . . . Stitch
> Walken!

Stitch Walken enters. He's drunk—and drinking shots that a waitress
places on stool before him. The audience is a combination of
conservative and hiply radical; the air is electrified. Stitch takes a
shot, chases it with beer, then apologizes:

> STITCH
> All right, so I'm drinking. How very <u>unprofessional</u>
> of me. Sorry: I got pressures. I'm only human.
> (pats himself)
> See? This is <u>real.</u> This ain't some guest shot on
> 'Church Windows'! Let's get into some trouble
> tonight, shall we? Let's talk about . . .
> (hums "Twilight Zone" theme)
> Senator Tony Kreutzer, he of the New Reality and
> the Messiah Complex. Sieg heil! Sieg <u>hologram</u>!
> Sieg <u>MimeCom</u>!

A Man in Suit exits; Paige notes this. Stitch has another shot. As his
monologue continues, the laughter dies down. The room becomes
polarized—the sympathetic and the scornful.

> STITCH
> Scary man, Senator K. Ever read his books? Pretty
> bad, even for sci-fi: all about old white guys who
> think they're God. Ring a bell?

Stitch's supporters AD LIB hoots and encouragement; a few of the
conservative types walk out.

> STITCH
> Hey, don't go! Don't leave—this is important!
> Heckle me, but don't walk out! We <u>elected</u> this
> man, that's what I can't understand. He <u>kills</u>
> people—we <u>let</u> him! The 'hospitals'—the ones
> they call Perceptories? Those aren't <u>hospitals</u> . . .

A row of Men in Suits enter. Many in audience note this, become
alarmed; begin to exit. Stitch downs a shot, oblivious. Paige is getting
nervous.

> PAIGE
> Harry, let's go.

(CONTINUED)

                              HARRY
              No. I want to hear this—

                              STITCH
              How many out there know someone who was
              grabbed off the street? Come on, people—talk
              about it or you'll be next! I know a guy who was
              grabbed off the <u>toilet.</u>
                          (laughs hilariously; losing it)
              True story! Sitting there, minding his own
              business. . . . Remember Tully Woiwode, the
              artist? The guy they blinded? He had a
              sister—beautiful girl. They blew her head off in
              Griffith Park!

Two of the Men in Suits take the stage and grab the comic—he
punches one of them out and runs free. Pandemonium breaks loose.
Harry grabs Paige, makes way to exit—they're separated.

EXT. UNDERGROUND CLUB—NIGHT

Chaos as patrons pour from club. There are half a dozen Range
Rovers waiting outside, with a phalanx of Men in Suits. Harry exits,
looks for Paige.

                              HARRY
              Paige! Paige!

He's grabbed by Man in Suit, cuffed in plastic hog ties, and led to
Rover.

                              HARRY
              What the hell is going on?
                          (angry)
              Who are you, the police? I'm an attorney!

Another Man in Suit approaches, holds Harry's hand up to
ASSOCIATE, showing the palm tattoo.

                            ASSOCIATE
                          (to Harry)
              Why didn't you say?

They clip off his cuffs and exit. As "arrests" continue in b.g., Harry
examines his palm tattoo, passport to immunity—something's starting
to click.

INT. WYCKOFF HOUSE—ENTRANCE HALL/DEN—NIGHT

Harry enters, dishevelled from the riot; rubs wrists from where he
was cuffed. He enters den: In its middle, incongruously, is a stall
shower. A WOMAN steps out, wrapping towel around her—holds
bar of soap to "camera." She speaks, the volume low:

                                                    (CONTINUED)

> WOMAN
> Stay fresh and tingly with . . . "Summer Storm."

Harry turns OFF TV—the image disappears. COTY is curled up on the sofa, shivering and crying.

> HARRY
> What's the matter, little man?

> COTY
> Mommy left—with a Japanese man.

> HARRY
> She what? When?

> COTY
> She—said I wasn't her son—that I'm bad—that I killed that fat man, with a knife—

> HARRY
> Where's Deirdre?

> COTY
> (cries)
> They took her. Dad, I'm scared!

> HARRY
> (holding him)
> Mommy's sick—she didn't mean the things she said. I'm here, Coty. Daddy's here! Everything's going to be okay. Just be brave, for a little while. I'll call Grammie. Be brave for me now?

> COTY
> (nods; sniffling)
> I love you, Daddy.

CAMERA PUSHES IN ON Coty, a huge scary smile spreading on his lips, right through the crocodile tears. Harry doesn't see. . . .

> FADE OUT.

<u>END OF ACT TWO</u>

ACT THREE

FADE IN:

INT. WYCKOFF HOUSE—MORNING

Josie stands at front door. Harry hands Coty a little travel bag, gives him a hug.

> HARRY
> Don't give Grandma too hard a time, okay?
> (to Josie)
> You'll let me know if you hear from her?

> JOSIE
> (nods)
> It'll all work out.

Josie and Coty exit.

INT. THERAPIST'S OFFICE—DAY

Tobias Schenkl taps pencil rhythmically on desk while Harry talks from the couch.

> HARRY
> Coty said she was with a man—maybe she's been seeing someone else all along. Who could blame her. . . . It's funny: I mean, I can deal with the domestic stuff, but—the club last night—there's something all . . . wrong about it. Those cops—whatever they were—when they saw the tattoo, they released me.

> TOBIAS
> You're certain that was the reason?

> HARRY
> The guy held my hand up for the other to see. Then, he looked at me and said, 'Why didn't you say?'—like I was one of them.

> TOBIAS
> Grace is unstable; she's taken your daughter—and you're talking about nightclubs!

> HARRY
> It's crazy, isn't it?

> TOBIAS
> You've got to go to the police—

(CONTINUED)

> HARRY
> Police? There <u>are</u> no police! Or maybe it's the other way around—there's nothing <u>but</u> police . . . I gotta go . . .

Harry CLICKS OFF the PICTURE PHONE, exits.

EXT. LITTLE TOKYO BATHHOUSE—NIGHT

ESTABLISHING SHOT.

INT. LITTLE TOKYO BATHHOUSE—BEDROOM—NIGHT

Grace and Eli watch Deirdre sleep; until Grace brought her to the bathhouse, he'd never seen his granddaughter.

> ELI
> Look at this tiny creature . . .

> GRACE
> Poor thing—she's exhausted. It's so hard, being taken away from everything familiar.

> ELI
> (to Deirdre)
> My heart's balled up in your hands; do with me what you will. You say she doesn't talk?

> GRACE
> No.

> ELI
> Strange little creature . . . No words can describe what's happened to the world; so the little one has no words.

> GRACE
> I heard ghost stories in Japan when I was little—about demons who stole children and took them to the mountains: 'kamigakushi.' When the children came back, they were dumb; they couldn't speak.

> ELI
> (imperious)
> No one stole this little fox.

Hiro appears at door. He slips his hand into Grace's.

> ELI
> She'll have a voice. Her words are waiting—great, moonlit armies. They will have their campaign.

EXT. LITTLE TOKYO BATHHOUSE—COURTYARD—NIGHT

(CONTINUED)

Grace and Hiro stroll in the moonlight.

> HIRO
> We have to move from here soon.

> GRACE
> What's happening?

> HIRO
> They almost killed Stitch last night. They took forty
> people out of that club—five bodies were dumped
> at Tully's old studio in Venice.

> GRACE
> Oh, God . . .

> HIRO
> There's no time anymore—your father thinks
> they're going to kill Chickie. We're going to break
> him out.

Hiro stops walking; kisses her. Grace kisses back deeply, then pulls away and begins to cry. In the following, SUBTITLED JAPANESE DIALOGUE is indicated by underlining.

> HIRO
> (kissing her)
> I've always burned for you.

> GRACE
> Don't . . . Stop!
> (backs away)
> I have a husband!
> (less convincing this time)
> I have a husband. . . .

She turns from him, runs back to building. We HOLD ON Hiro.

EXT. WILD PALMS—NIGHT

ESTABLISHING SHOT.

INT. WILD PALMS—DINING ROOM—NIGHT

The Senator, Paige, Josie, Tabba and Coty sit at dinner—Paige and Coty beside each other, with Coty and the Senator at table's ends. Paige seems listless, disaffected. Servants appear and disappear, refilling glasses, etc.

> SENATOR
> (to Josie, cold)
> I want Chickie moved.

> JOSIE
> To where?

(CONTINUED)

                        SENATOR
Anywhere. Just do it. And I'm leaving it to you to
find Grace. It's a little late in the day to have your
neurotic daughter gum up the works.

                        TABBA
I have got to stop eating. I look like Cass Elliot.

                        COTY
Don't get crazy, Tabba.

                        TABBA
When you're in people's living rooms the way I
am, they can literally see the bloat.

The Senator looks at Paige, who's been pushing her food around on
the plate.

                        SENATOR
Earth to Paige!
            (as she looks up)
Any general insights to share with the group?

                        PAIGE
None. Sorry.

                        SENATOR
You were at the club with Harry—hope at least
you enjoyed the show. Funny man, Stitch Walken.

                        COTY
            (droll)
People are dying to see his act.

                        SENATOR
            (laughs)
This is one brutal kid I got! Come on, Paige, tell
me about it. Any good jokes?

                        PAIGE
I'm not a big fan of comedy.

                        COTY
She wasn't paying attention—too busy drooling
over Harry.
            (to Paige)
You're really pathetic.

Paige slaps Coty, startling everyone. The slap doesn't seem brutal; we
should feel it was well-placed and long coming—appropriate. Coty
looks stunned, then starts to cry.

                        PAIGE
Don't you ever talk to me that way, do you
understand? Ever!

                                        (CONTINUED)

Coty runs from the table—an awkward silence. As the Senator speaks, he stands and walks to Coty's empty chair, where he sits.

> SENATOR
> She's the only one that can really get to
> him—guess that's the way it's supposed to be.
>   (beat)
> In a few weeks, I'll be announcing my candidacy
> for President. Monday, the Wild Palms Group will
> issue a terse press release. It will read: 'Senator
> Tony Kreutzer of California has announced his
> engagement and imminent marriage to longtime
> aide, Paige Katz.'

He puts his hand on Paige's; she stiffens, suppressing her horror.

> SENATOR
> Let us pray:

> ALL
> The wind is old and still at play, While I must
> hurry upon my way . . .

INT. SYNTHIOTICS HOUSE—MEETING ROOM—DAY

Harry stands in a circle of men and women, their arms linked. Behind them, a banner stretches across wall: NEWCOMERS "MIXERS" BRUNCH—WELCOME SYNTHIOTICS! Enroll Preschool Now. All heads are bowed—except Harry's. He looks uncomfortable, as if he wished he wasn't there. He affectlessly mouths the words:

> HARRY AND OTHERS
> . . . For I am running to Paradise.
>   (beat)
> Korede ikimasho! Banzai!

Everyone pats each other's shoulders vigorously; Harry smiles emptily—he isn't "with" it anymore.

EXT. SYNTHIOTICS HOUSE—DAY

Harry exits onto street. He pauses, turns to look in window of New Realism bookstore that fronts the building, graced by a large blow-up of the Senator. Lining the window are two of the Senator's bestsellers: Confessions of a Go Master and Wild Psalms. Harry turns back to street—he looks lost, deflated. All around him, sunny Synthiotics people hand out literature to passersby. Harry begins to walk, and is approached by filthy BEGGAR.

> BEGGAR
> I'm a homeless survivor of the disaster in Boca
> Raton—
>   (as Harry hands him bills)
> Thank you! Bless you, sir!

(CONTINUED)

Harry walks away; the Beggar catches up, putting his hand on him. Harry turns around, irritated.

> HARRY
> (testy)
> That's all I have—
> (in disbelief)
> Tommy?

> TOMMY
> (furtive)
> Act like you're being hassled . . .

> HARRY
> What's going on?

> TOMMY
> Grace and Deirdre are safe . . .

> HARRY
> Where are they?

> TOMMY
> Can't tell you that.

A patrol car slowly passes by. Harry reaches in his pocket again, as if to give Tommy a handout. The car passes.

> TOMMY
> Meet me Sunday at noon, Court of Psalms—the cemetery.

> HARRY
> Do you need any money?

> TOMMY
> (smiles warmly)
> No. But thanks—old friend. Remember that story you used to love about me robbing houses when we were kids?

> HARRY
> You only stole the mirrors—

> TOMMY
> I'm putting them all back, now: flowers for you, Harry—a bouquet of looking-glasses. So, see what you can see—for old times.

Tommy scurries off; the manic gait of the disenfranchised. Harry watches . . .

INT. WYCKOFF HOUSE—DAY

(CONTINUED)

Harry enters the darkened house. He opens curtain, peers out to back yard—sees something. Exits.

EXT. WYCKOFF HOUSE—BACK YARD—DAY

Paige Katz lays on a chaise lounge beside emptied pool. She smokes and wears sunglasses; her face is puffy from crying. Harry sits beside her—she turns her face away.

> PAIGE
> Don't look at me.

> HARRY
> What are you doing here?

> PAIGE
> I need to talk.

> HARRY
> You want a drink?

> PAIGE
> No—I want to do this sober.

> HARRY
> I'm listening.

> PAIGE
> The Senator entered politics in the late Seventies. Back then, my father was a well-respected journalist; to him, the Senator was a dangerous man, a demagogue. He wrote a series of articles tying Kreutzer and Synthiotics to a shadowy vigilante group—it cost the Senator the election. Men broke into the house and took me away. I was three years old—

> HARRY
> The Fathers . . .

> PAIGE
> I never saw my parents again; I was raised in New Realist foster homes.

> HARRY
> (incredulous)
> Everything you told me: your husband, your lost little boy—

> PAIGE
> Lies.

> HARRY
> Why, Paige?

(CONTINUED)

                    PAIGE
To pull you in.

                    HARRY
Are you with him . . . now?
          (as she nods)
In college—when we first met—

                    PAIGE
They were grooming me to be his wife, even then.
He was jealous of you—that's why they sent me
away. That's why they brought Grace in. . . .

                    HARRY
What are you saying?

                    PAIGE
Your marriage was arranged—two royal families!
Josie is the Senator's sister!

                    HARRY
          (roughly lifts her)
Why did you do this to me!?

                    PAIGE
They did it—

                    HARRY
Is Coty my son?

                    PAIGE
          (hysterical)
What they did to that poor little boy! What they
did!

                    HARRY
Answer me, Paige! Is Coty my son?

                    PAIGE
I'm wading through blood, Harry! I am drowning!

                    HARRY
Who is he, Paige? Answer me!

                    PAIGE
God help me!

                    HARRY
Answer me!

He slaps her.

> PAIGE
> He's mine! I had him with the Senator! He was
> switched with your baby, at birth! Stolen—the
> way they stole my life!

CAMERA PUSHES IN ON Harry, staggered. He throws her back
down on chaise, exits.

EXT. MARINA—YACHT—DAY

Harry runs down dock and over gangway to gleaming white yacht,
The Floating World. He's greeted by men in blue blazers with Wild
Palms insignias. Josie, in stylish caftan, waves from prow.

> JOSIE
> Harry!

Harry comes aboard.

THE FLOATING WORLD

A frantic Harry rushes to her; Josie's relaxed and smiling, as yet
unaware of her son-in-law's agitation.

> JOSIE
> This is a surprise. I thought you and water didn't
> mix—

> HARRY
> Where's Coty?

> JOSIE
> Napping—down below. What's wrong? Did you
> hear from Grace?

> HARRY
> I'm taking him home.

> JOSIE
> What for?

> HARRY
> He belongs with me.

> JOSIE
> I hate resorting to cliché, but you look like you
> saw a ghost.

> HARRY
> I did—Paige Katz.

> JOSIE
> You know what, Harry? The women in your life
> are really going to hell.

(CONTINUED)

                              HARRY
            And you're driving the bus!

Men in blazers hover menacingly in b.g.

                              JOSIE
            Don't you dare get righteous with me—not now!
            You wanted this life; you begged for it! Did you
            think there wasn't a price to pay? Did you think
            it's all about beach houses and Hockney
            lithographs? About fooling around on your wife? Is
            that what you thought, Harry?

                              HARRY
            Grace tried to warn me—

                              JOSIE
            Count yourself lucky! I never wanted you to marry
            her—it was the Senator's idea. Because of that
            marriage, you're going to be an historical figure; a
            rich one, at that.

                              HARRY
            I want to see Coty—

                              JOSIE
            Let it go, Harry! Let it go!

The men in blazers prevent Harry from going below—Harry punches
one of them out. They leap on him, hold him down.

                              JOSIE
            Get off him!

They jump off, like trained dogs. Harry stands, roughly shoves one
aside. He looks at Josie a beat, exits to stairs.

                              JOSIE
                         (to self, sotto)
            Go below, Harry—because nothing matters.
            You're with us now. . . .

INT. THE FLOATING WORLD—LOWER DECK—DAY

Harry enters the richly wooded lower deck. Attractive young men
and women in sea-blue caftans softly murmur—Harry makes his way
through them, towards the stateroom.

                              VOICES
            The palm at the end of the mind, beyond the last
            thought rises in the bronze decor. A goldfeathered
            bird sings in the palm, without human meaning.
            Without human feeling, a foreign song . . .

                                                  (CONTINUED)

He enters a stateroom. More men and women—older, with darker caftans, embroidered with gold.

                    VOICES
          The palm stands on the edge of space. The wind
          moves slowly in the branches. The bird's fire-
          fangled feathers dangle down.

Without a cue, the men and women kneel, touching their foreheads to floor in silent prostration. The little boy on the dais has had his back to all—suddenly, chillingly, Coty turns, looks at Harry. Smiles.

                                        FADE OUT.

          END OF ACT THREE

ACT FOUR

FADE IN:

EXT. HOLLYWOOD CEMETERY—DAY

Harry parks beside mausoleum marked Court of Psalms. He rounds corner—"drawers" of graves. He sits on bench and fidgets; stands, walks to wall of graves. Walks slowly along, looking at them. Something catches his eye:

DEX WYCKOFF—b. 1943 d. 1972. "Father and Friend"

Staggered, he runs his finger along its raised letters.

> HARRY
> (sotto)
Father . . .

ANGLE ON PAIR OF RATTY SNEAKERS

TILT to reveal PETER, the Maps to Stars boy, entering mausoleum space.

> PETER
> Tourists like to come here—they're real morbid.
> It's worse than Day of the Locust.

> HARRY
> You never told me your name.

> PETER
> Peter. I know yours.

> HARRY
> Where do you live?

> PETER
> In the tunnels.
> (extends his hand)
> I'll take you to Tommy. . . .
> (as they start to walk)
> We're off to see the wizards. What do you need,
> Harry? A heart? A brain? Courage?

> HARRY
> I'll take a helping of each. . . .

Peter takes Harry's hand and leads him from mausoleum.

EXT. MUNICIPAL POOL—ENTRANCE—DAY

An old, abandoned public pool. Josie pulls up in limo. Armed men escort her from car while her driver's frisked for weapons. She holds

(CONTINUED)

a long-stemmed rose. Then Josie is frisked; someone takes the rose from her, but hands it back. She's led inside.

SWIMMING POOL AREA

More armed men with walkie-talkies, ringing the enormous, empty pool. Josie's led to stairs of shallow end. Eli Levitt stands beside table and chairs, at deep end; wine, glasses and fine white linen. She walks to him unescorted. When she reaches him, they nod, but don't touch—tension and awkwardness between the former marrieds.

                    ELI
          Hello, Josie.

                    JOSIE
          Hello, Eli. I missed you.

                    ELI
                  (ironic)
          So did a lot of other people.

                    JOSIE
                  (genuine)
          I'm truly sorry.

                    ELI
          Sit down.

They sit, he pours wine.

                    JOSIE
          Thank you. I thought it was time to . . . make
          amends. I never stopped loving you; I'm not
          ashamed to admit it.

                    ELI
          Sounds a little like a Channel Three soap, no?

                    JOSIE
          I expect you to be bitter.

                    ELI
          What largesse. Ten years locked up, Josie. You
          murdered my wife, robbed me of my child. . . .

                    JOSIE
          I had nothing to do with that! She _wasn't_ your
          wife—that was bigamy! We were never legally
          divorced!

                    ELI
          You kidnap and torture my son—funny way to
          show love, isn't it?

                                        (CONTINUED)

                    JOSIE
    We are _epic_—two generals who happen to be on
    opposing sides. It was always that way with us,
    even in bed. A holy war; that's why it was so
    good. I did what I had to.

                    ELI
    What do we do now, Josie? Settle down in the
    suburbs and barbecue by the pool? Fly to Vegas
    and get hitched, like Elvis and Priscilla? Why the
    reunion, Josie?

                    JOSIE
    I'll tell you why. Because . . . I am parched. My
    brother loves the desert, not I: I want the flood. To
    touch you, taste you . . . smell you. To start the
    holy war all over again—

He stands, goes to her, lifts her from chair—she's helpless. He kisses
her deeply.

                    ELI
    Release Chickie—or there's nothing to talk about.

This time, she kisses him—hungrily.

                    JOSIE
    I'll give you Chickie . . .
                (more kisses)
    for Grace.

He smiles at her, sly. She smiles back. He kisses her, then bites her
lip. She screams, stumbling away in pain. He moves on her, grabs
her; whispers intently in her ear as she cringes at his words.

                    ELI
    You're no general! You're a mercenary—a
    cannibal! A pimp, with the wings of a bat! I never
    wanted you—any part of you!

Bloodied and humiliated, she storms from the pool. SUBTITLED
Japanese:

                    JOSIE
    You will pay! You will pay!

EXT. MUNICIPAL POOL—ENTRANCE—DAY

Josie, holding her bloody mouth, dashes to limo. CAMERA PANS TO
Harry and Peter, watching from hidden vantage. They head for pool
once she's pulled away.

INT. TUNNELS UNDER MUNICIPAL POOL—DAY

Harry kneels, hugs Deirdre; then stands and embraces Grace. They

                                        (CONTINUED)

kiss, while Peter watches. Tommy, Woiwode, Eli, Stitch and Aides mingle.

> HARRY
> Forgive me, Grace!

> GRACE
> It doesn't matter—now that you're here.

> WOIWODE
> He thought it was all a dream!

> TOMMY
> I told you one day you'd wake up at the watering hole.

> ELI
> Tomorrow, we're going to the desert: we're gonna set the palms on fire!

A woman's SCREAMS ECHO from down tunnel: an Aide with walkie-talkie runs to Eli.

> AIDE
> We found her in the pool—we were about to flood.

Paige Katz enters, held by more Aides; gagged now. Grace and Harry react—Paige deliberately avoids looking at them.

> ELI
> Was she alone?

> AIDE
> We're checking the perimeters.

> ELI
> (removes her gag)
> How'd you find us?

> PAIGE
> The boy gave me a map—

Peter hears this, bolts down tunnel; Aides chase after him. Eli stops them.

> WOIWODE
> (sniffing)
> I smell Paige Katz. Unmistakable—the smell of sea breeze, skunk and . . . <u>death.</u>

If he could only see to lay hands on her; Tommy holds Woiwode back.

(CONTINUED)

                         PAIGE
They moved your son.

                          ELI
                        (cool)
Oh?

                         PAIGE
The Senator knows your plans—he had Chickie
moved from the desert to a safe house in
Hollywood: the place they killed Gavin
Whitehope.

                         GRACE
Liar! She's lying!

                         STITCH
                   (mock disbelief)
The bride of Frankenstein, a <u>liar</u>? Say it isn't so!

                         PAIGE
I'm telling the truth!

                          ELI
What do you think, Harry? Is she telling the truth?

                         HARRY
                   (a beat, then)
I believe her.

Grace storms off.

                         PAIGE
There's more: At four o'clock, the Senator's going
to 'interview' your son personally—he thinks
Chickie has some kind of techno-shamanistic key
to eternity. Kreutzer said he'd tear the secret from
Chickie's bones, if he had to.

                          ELI
Less than an hour. You'll take us to this safe
house, Ms. Katz. And if I do not come away with
my son, we will surely gut you on the street.

Bustle as Eli takes Harry aside, arm around his shoulder.

                         HARRY
I'm going with you—

                          ELI
No! Go to the Senator. You haven't seen him
since that business on the yacht with Coty—he's
probably worried about your allegiance. Renew it!
Keep him from his appointment with my son.
                        (MORE)

                                              (CONTINUED)

ELI (CONT'D)
He'll bring too many with him; we won't have a
chance. Be our Trojan horse, Harry. And
remember: There are no politics. Only fathers and
beach houses!

Paige approaches the wounded Grace.

PAIGE
I'm sorry, Grace. For everything.

Grace smiles, then slaps Paige hard in the face; Paige doesn't strike
back.

Woiwode, Stitch and Aides tend to Tommy, who's bent over and
sick—his nose is bleeding a little; bleeding blue fluid.

STITCH
It's the Mimezine . . .

WOIWODE
(to Tommy)
Maybe you should stay behind. With me—

TOMMY
No—that is not going to happen! I'm going with
them!

Harry approaches Grace and Deirdre; Grace can't look him in the
face.

HARRY
Eli says the tunnels aren't safe. Take Deirdre and
go to the house—they won't think to look for you
there. I'll come tonight.

He takes her head in his hands, forcing her to look at his eyes. She
softens. He kisses her cheek.

ELI
Flood the pool! We're moving out!

EXT. WILD PALMS—ROCK GARDEN/POOL—DAY

Harry and the Senator are separated by the expanse of the Zen
garden.

SENATOR
You don't seriously believe Coty belongs to
someone else, do you, Harry?

HARRY
No.

(CONTINUED)

                              SENATOR
Who started that delightful little rumor?

                              HARRY
Grace.

                              SENATOR
An <u>unstable</u> woman . . . that kind of hysteria is
often contagious. Divorce her, Harry—make it
official; unburden yourself.
                              (beat)
Wild Palms has big plans, and you're a part of
them. Everything's got to run smoothly now. Is my
marriage to Paige going to be a problem?

                              HARRY
Why should it?

                              SENATOR
It's tough to put out an old flame.
                              (beat)
I withheld certain things from you because you
would not understand—nothing "Machiavellian"
about it.

                              HARRY
I'm with you. Let me be like a son.

                              SENATOR
Talk to the boy—talk to Coty.
                              (embraces Harry)
'For this, thy brother was dead, and is alive again;
and was lost, and is found.'

EXT. IVAR TERRACE MOTEL—DAY

Six vans filled with armed men pull into parking lot.

INT. ONE OF VANS—DAY

Eli Levitt, Tommy Laszlo and Stitch Walken hold weapons in
readiness. In back seat, Woiwode holds knife to throat of Paige Katz.

EXT. WYCKOFF HOUSE—BACK YARD—DAY

In the drained pool, Grace, Deirdre and Peter move furtively toward
house. Winds blow the palms.

INT. IVAR TERRACE MOTEL—DAY

A nurse and guards. Chickie lays in bed, pale and perspiry; breath
labored and shallow. The nurse fits an oxygen mask on his face as
guard turns up "HOUSE OF THE RISING SUN" on bedside RADIO.
GUNFIRE from outside; the guards barely have time to register it
when Eli, Stitch, Tommy and others burst into room and quickly kill

                                                    (CONTINUED)

them. Eli rushes to his son, who looks frightened and confused.

> ELI
> It's all right, baby boy! We're gonna take you
> home.

> CHICKIE
> Terra? Terra?

> ELI
> It's Daddy. . . .

> STITCH
> Eli, come on! Let's go!

> ELI
> We're taking you to the water—can you hold on?

Chickie nods; they gather him up, carry him out.

INT. WILD PALMS—LIVING ROOM—DAY

Harry and the Senator enter from terrace. Coty also enters, from back
rooms. He wears colorful robes and is escorted by half a dozen
acolytes—young men and women in caftans. The smiling Coty goes
straight to Harry.

> COTY
> You know what I love? I love the men who slash
> paintings of the old masters. See the palms out
> there, Harry, shivering against the blue skies? The
> simple mysticism of a windy day . . . Know what I
> told the Senator? I said, 'Today is a day for
> unicorns.'

The acolytes gently make Harry kneel before the boy.

> COTY
> You were good to me—but I'm not that boy
> anymore. Those 'Father Knows Best' days are
> gone—only Fathers know best.

He leans over, kissing Harry tenderly on the cheek.

> COTY
> It's a wise father that knows his own child.
> (whispers in Harry's ear)
> There are so many enemies on the way to the
> garden. . . .

INT./EXT. IVAR TERRACE MOTEL—DAY

Eli and Stitch carry Chickie to van. Tommy follows, covering them by
FIRING at pursuers. When Tommy nears the van, he suddenly looks
disoriented—he falls to ground.

(CONTINUED)

TOMMY'S POV

Awed and terrified, his hand reaches out, trembling, to touch something as yet unseen. PULL BACK to reveal Tommy no longer at motel setting—rather, he lays beside the stony gothic facade of a great cathedral; touches its smooth surface.

BACK TO VAN

Eli and Stitch load Chickie in. Paige watches nervously from back seat, Woiwode's knife still held to her neck, where she bleeds a little. Woiwode is agitated.

> WOIWODE
> Where's Tommy?!

> STITCH
> He's coming—

Stitch turns to look—sees Tommy laying on ground, arm extended to unseen church. Stitch exits van, goes to him.

> STITCH
> Tommy, come on!

He hustles Tommy to van—where Friends help him to back seat, beside Woiwode. Stitch is climbing in himself when he's SHOT in the back. He seems to laugh for a moment, as if he's heard a joke—then gasps horribly.

> TOMMY
> No!

They try to pull Stitch in, but the GUNFIRE is heavy and Men in Suits advance.

> ELI
> (to driver)
> Move! Move! Move!

As the VAN SCREECHES off, the motel GUN BATTLE CONTINUES. They leave Stitch behind.

INT. WYCKOFF HOUSE—MASTER BEDROOM—DAY

CAMERA ON framed family photo. Harry, Grace, Deirdre and Coty. We PAN TO Grace and Deirdre; Deirdre lays on bed—for the first time we remember, she's crying.

> GRACE
> Cry, my baby. Let it go—it's gonna be all right.
> Everything's going to be all right. . . .

Peter watches from doorway. A sudden NOISE downstairs makes him turn head nervously; as does Grace.

(CONTINUED)

> GRACE
> (calling out)

Harry?

EXT. BEACH/RUINED NIGHTCLUB—DAY

Hysteria in cramped van as they reach old On the Rox Komedy Klub. Chickie is fading in Eli's arms. Tommy's distraught.

> TOMMY

He came back for me, Tully!

> WOIWODE

It's all right—

> TOMMY

We can't just leave him there, man! We gotta go back!

> ELI

Shut up, Tommy! Everyone shut up!

EXT. BEACH—DAY

The van pulls onto sand. Eli and Paige carry Chickie to water, leaving behind Woiwode to comfort the wailing Tommy.

> ELI

We're here, baby boy! See? We're at the water. . . .

> CHICKIE

Is it real?

> ELI
> (crying)

Remember how Mama always brought you to the ocean when you got sick?

> CHICKIE

Where's the orchestra?
> (as Paige watches, crying softly now)
I hear a symphony—

He dies. Eli howls to the skies with rage and horror as he holds him—a Pieta.

INT. WYCKOFF HOUSE—MASTER BEDROOM—DAY

Harry enters the ransacked bedroom. A picture frame on the ground. He picks it up: the family photo seen earlier, its glass shattered and blood smeared.

> HARRY

N-n-n-n-n-n-n-n-o-o-o-o-o-o!

(CONTINUED)

EXT. LITTLE TOKYO BATHHOUSE—DAY

A Range Rover pulls up; a body's thrown out—Grace. Still alive. Bathhouse attendants scurry to her aid.

INT. WILD PALMS—DEN—DAY

Tabba sits on sofa, chewing gum. The Senator's head hangs low as he sits in his chair, oblivious to a holosynth: Chap Starfall is singing "All Along the Watchtower."

> TABBA
> Hate to say it, but I like him so much better since he died—that 'posthumous' quality really makes me shiver.

An Aide enters, whispers in the Senator's ear. The Senator nods; Aide exits. The Senator turns OFF TV—the sumo images disappear. After a beat, the door opens—and Deirdre shyly enters.

> TABBA
> Hi, Deirdre! C'mere! It's Auntie Tabba.

She goes to her.

> SENATOR
> (to unseen man)
> Any problems?

> VOICE (O.S.)
> No.

> TABBA
> (hugging Deirdre)
> What sweetness you are! What sweetness!

> VOICE (O.S.)
> Will you need me for anything else?

> SENATOR
> No.

The CAMERA PANS SLOWLY TO unseen man—Dr. Tobias Schenkl.

> SENATOR
> Good night, Tobias. Thank you.

Tobias nods, exits.

FADE OUT.

THE END

WILD PALMS

Fifth Hour

"Hungry Ghosts"

ACT ONE

FADE IN:

EXT. WILD PALMS—NIGHT

ESTABLISHING SHOT. The palms, blown by winds.

WILD PALMS COURTYARD

An orchestra. PAIGE, in wedding dress, and the SENATOR, in Edwardian tux, dance to "You Are the Sunshine of My Life." COTY, also in tux, films them with an odd-looking device—the MimeCam. The Senator is exuberant; Paige smiles emptily.

Among those watching: HARRY, JOSIE and TABBA. As the dancing couple sweeps by applauding guests, Paige catches Harry's eye. He smiles back flatly, exits.

ZEN GARDEN AREA—POOL

Harry gets himself a drink at the bar. He's approached by a cop—LIEUTENANT ROBERT GRINDROD.

> LIEUTENANT GRINDROD
> Heard from your wife, Harry?

> HARRY
> Who are you?

> LIEUTENANT GRINDROD
> (almost ingenuous)
> I'm sorry—poor habit of mine.
> (extends hand)
> Lieutenant Bob Grindrod.

> HARRY
> (doesn't take the hand)
> Working the wedding beat?

> LIEUTENANT GRINDROD
> (laughs)
> The Senator and I are old friends. Just where do you think she is, Harry? You must have thought about it—maybe even hired someone to track her down.

(CONTINUED)

> HARRY
> Grace is in Japan. Soon as I know where, I'll go
> over.

> LIEUTENANT GRINDROD
> I think she's with her daddy. I think Eli Levitt's
> done a real number on her—Patty Hearst-style.
> Dangerous man. And not a great situation for the
> little girl—Deirdre. That's her name, isn't it,
> Harry?

COURTYARD

Many couples on dance floor now. We TRACK WITH Paige and the
Senator as they waltz. He caresses the mark left on her neck by Tully
Woiwode's blade.

> SENATOR
> The audacity of Tully Woiwode! Holding my
> lovely bride-to-be hostage with a stiletto, like so
> much terrorist-fodder. You were a hostage,
> weren't you, darling?

> PAIGE
> What's that supposed to mean?

> SENATOR
> It's all just too horrible to think of! There was poor
> Tully, back in the catbird seat, heart revving
> furiously as he imagined carving up the gorgeous
> neck of his beloved sister's assassin, yet . . .
> something held him back. What do you think that
> was, Paige?

> PAIGE
> Tully's never been a killer. Besides, he always
> respected you—it's Josie he hates.

Josie cuts in, holds the Senator in dance position. Coty tracks them
with the MimeCam.

> JOSIE
> (mock jealous)
> All right, Paige: You've had him long enough!

> SENATOR
> Fred and Ginger time.

> JOSIE
> (to Coty)
> Mr. DeMille? I'm ready for my closeup!

Josie and the Senator dance off, Paige watching.

POOL/ZEN GARDEN AREAS

Harry and the Lieutenant wander away from the bar. We sense that Harry would like to shake this asshole.

> LIEUTENANT GRINDROD
> I've had a helluva time keeping you out of the press.

> HARRY
> I didn't know you cared.

> LIEUTENANT GRINDROD
> MimeCom's about to go public: Your various affiliations don't exactly make you employee-of-the-month material!

> HARRY
> Can I share something with you, Grindrod? I'm feeling a definite urge to seriously slap you around. Why don't you just crawl back to whatever wet hole you call home?

He exits.

> LIEUIENANT GRINDROD
> (after him)
> The Senator's the best friend you got, Harry! Anyone else would have thrown you to the dogs a long time ago!

OFF COURTYARD

Paige smokes a cigarette in the night air. Harry approaches, agitated—almost out of control.

> PAIGE
> I was looking for you. . . .

> HARRY
> He knows where they are—

> PAIGE
> What are you talking about?

> HARRY
> Deirdre and Grace—that sonofabitchin' lieutenant knows! He was playing with me; watching me squirm! He's probably holding them somewhere right here on the grounds—like they did Chickie!

> PAIGE
> Harry, calm down—

                              HARRY
                        (laughs; near hysteria)
          Calm down! The woman who just married the
          antichrist tells me to calm down!

                              PAIGE
          I don't think they've been hurt—I'm trying to find
          out what happened. . . .

                              HARRY
          Why hasn't Tommy gotten a hold of me? Why
          hasn't someone <u>called</u>?

                              PAIGE
          It'll be all right!

                              HARRY
                           (baffled)
          If they knew Grace and Deirdre were waiting for
          me back at the house—if they knew <u>that much</u>,
          they must have known I was <u>involved</u>! They'll be
          coming after <u>me</u> next—

                              PAIGE
          Harry, stop it!

                              HARRY
          Are you with them, Paige? You killed for
          them—how many, Paige?

She tries to exit; he grabs her.

                              HARRY
          Am I next? Why don't you just do me right here?

                              PAIGE
          Harry, please!

                              HARRY
                           (laughs)
          I'm really freaking—it's all starting to hit me.
                           (serious)
          Gotta do something . . . maybe kill the Senator—

                              PAIGE
          Don't get crazy! Let it settle, or you'll lose
          everything!

COURTYARD

The Senator, with Coty beside him, talks over the band's mike; he
holds the odd-looking camera Coty had earlier.

                                                    (CONTINUED)

                            SENATOR
        I want to play a little something for you we just
        taped with the new MimeCam—

                             COTY
        I taped it!

                            SENATOR
        He taped it.
                          (laughter)
        It's portable; costs about the same as a black-
        market pancreas.
                          (laughter)
        We'll have it on the market sometime in the
        fall—ladies and gentlemen, forget about instant
        replay: welcome to instant relive!

Suddenly the Senator and Paige appear, in holosynth, doing wedding
dance that Coty taped at top of act. Eerie and beautiful; the crowd
roars its approval. An aide bends over, his ear to the Senator.

                            SENATOR
                           (sotto)
        Where's Paige?

Coty sets the MimeCam down on table, then runs mischievous circles
around the holosynth couple.

OFF COURTYARD

Harry and Paige watch the ghostly dance.

                             PAIGE
        I've got to go back in.

She squeezes his arm, exits. We HOLD ON him a beat, disconsolate.

COURTYARD

Lieutenant Grindrod whispers into the Senator's ear. The Senator
stands, exits. The holo-couple continue their dance. In the half-
darkness, Coty goes back to table to retrieve MimeCam—it's gone.

BUILDING OF CAPTIVE—NIGHT

The Senator and Lieutenant ENTER FRAME. A mud-spattered RANGE
ROVER with black-tinted windows IDLES there.

                            SENATOR
        What do you have?

                     LIEUTENANT GRINDROD
        Gavin Whitehope's kid—picked him up in
        Barstow, on his way to the Wilderzone. He's the
                           (MORE)

                                                      (CONTINUED)

>   LIEUTENANT GRINDROD (CONT'D)
>   one who leaked Chickie's move to the motel.
>   (beat)
>   It wasn't Paige.

The Senator walks to the car; the back window rolls down a few inches. He addresses the person in the car.

>   SENATOR
>   Bury him.

REVERSE SHOT

TOBIAS SCHENKL nods, then signals to the driver. The car pulls away, into the night.

EXT. DESERT—DAY

Windmills turning. A billboard reads: WHO SAID "ALMOST" DOESN'T COUNT? MIMECOM—LEADERS IN TELEPRESENCE.

Three kids on bikes. They pedal furiously, toward something stuck in the sand in b.g. Spokes turning. Panting. The curious kids get closer.

CAMERA is BEHIND the buried thing as the kids approach, slowing down. We hear the BUZZ of FLIES. The kids stop fifteen feet from it, stare. CAMERA DOLLIES AROUND to reveal rhinoceros head, lifelike, yet clearly made from papier-mâché. It is stuck over whatever is buried there. Fresh dirt is packed down around it; the immediate soil is darkly stained. The ROAR now, of FLIES. One of the braver kids moves closer. His hand reaches for the edge of the head, and starts to push it off . . . Gavin Whitehope, Jr.

EXT. DEL-MAR THEATRE—DAY

Harry pulls up in his 'Vette, parks. He holds up a Map to the Stars—scrawled on it is the message, "MEET ME DEL-MAR THEATRE—THURS. MATINEE." He gets out of the car, takes in the double-bill marquee: REBEL WITHOUT A CAUSE and KWAIDAN. He goes to ticket booth.

INT. DEL-MAR THEATRE—DAY

Harry's eyes adjust to the light as he fumbles to seat.

Onscreen is the sequence where Sal Mineo, James Dean and Natalie Wood are at a deserted mansion: Mineo leads them by candlelight into the large, empty swimming pool—a familiar image.

PETER leans over from seat behind, startling him a moment; still, Harry doesn't have to look to know who it is.

(CONTINUED)

                          PETER
            This is my favorite part—I always think they're
            gonna go down underneath the pool, like the
            Friends!

                          HARRY
            Do you know where my wife and daughter are?

                          PETER
            No one watches movies anymore—only T.V. Look
            at how happy Plato is—he thinks Natalie Wood
            and James Dean are his mom and dad!

                          HARRY
            Peter . . . are they still alive?

                          PETER
            Deirdre's with the Fathers, somewhere in the
            desert.

                          HARRY
            And Grace?

                          PETER
            The Wilderzone—Toshiba Park.

                          HARRY
            Take me to her.

As they exit, Natalie Wood and James Dean cover up the sleeping
Sal Mineo—like covering up the dead.

INT. SUBWAY—DAY

The dispossessed, furtive and impoverished seem to stare Harry
down. A dirty, sandaled hippie with guitar stands at end of car and
sings: "Small Circle of Friends."

Advertisements inside car read, GET ME TO THE CHURCH ON
TIME. CHURCH WINDOWS. 8 O'CLOCK, ON WPN and KREUTZER
FOR PRESIDENT—WHAT DREAMS ARE MADE OF and FREE
SUNDAY LECTURES, CHURCH OF SYNTHIOTICS. Over all, varied
graffiti: "Chickie Levitt Died For Your Sins," "Everything Must Go"
("Go" slashed out, replaced with "come"), "Pray for the Stolen
Children."

EXT. WILDERZONE—DAY

A multicultural frontiersland. Peter pulls the stolen MimeCam from
his backpack, records goings-on while leading Harry through forest of
neon, street stalls and cacophonous MUSIC—to a bar called the
Hungry Ghost. A banner above it reads: WE HAVE HOLO-
KARAOKE!

INT. HUNGRY GHOST—DAY

                                                           (CONTINUED)

Peter and Harry enter. A seedy place where you can get sushi or hamburgers. Jukebox. TULLY WOIWODE calls to them from booth—he wears stylish glasses with metallic lenses. Peter exits.

                    WOIWODE
          Harold!

                    HARRY
          Tully?

                    WOIWODE
          Come on down!

                    HARRY
          Can you see?

                    WOIWODE
          I do all right.
                    (indicates glasses)
          They're hardwired into the cortex. Sit down—you
          look awful!

                    HARRY
          Where's Grace?

                    WOIWODE
          Eli doesn't want to take the chance.

                    HARRY
          Dammit, Tully, where is she!

                    WOIWODE
          Maybe in a week—

                    HARRY
          Is Grace all right?

                    WOIWODE
          She's fine.
                    (shouts)
          Choko, can we get some Scotch here?

                    HARRY
          What happened that night?

                    WOIWODE
          They took Deirdre; left Grace for dead at the old
          bathhouse. We patched her up like new. So stop
          worrying.
                    (looks around)
          How do you like the club?

                    HARRY
                    (deadpan)
          Fabulous.

                                              (CONTINUED)

                                        WOIWODE
The Wilderzone has its own laws—cops stay
away. Easy for a blind artist and his fugitive
friends to blend in.

                                        HARRY
Look: I know what Grace was going
through—why she was cracking up. I can't sit by
anymore—

                                        WOIWODE
What do you want to do, Harry? Throw molotovs?
                                        (shouts)
Hey, Choko! <u>Sumimasen!</u>

Woiwode laughs as TOMMY enters. Tommy trembles. He looks
macabre, as if he hasn't slept in a week; a forced jauntiness makes
the effect even worse. During following, CHOKO—obese and
taciturn—enters with drinks, exits.

                                        TOMMY
Look who's here—stranger in a strange land!

He embraces Harry.

                                        HARRY
                                        (warm)
I didn't think I'd see you again.
                                        (concerned)
You okay?

                                        TOMMY
Never better.

                                        WOIWODE
He's been partying.

                                        TOMMY
Partying is <u>such</u> sweet sorrow. Not exactly your
part of the neighborhood, Harry—welcome to the
Fourth World!

Tommy dabs his nose with a white handkerchief—blue fluid leaves
its mark.

                                        TOMMY
Hey, Choko, I'm starving. Cook me up something,
woman!
                                        (to Harry)
Good to see you, Harry. Stick around—the
place'll grow on you! Choko!

As quickly as he appeared, Tommy reels away.

                                                        (CONTINUED)

> HARRY
> What's the matter with him?

> WOIWODE
> Mimezine sickness—he's not responding to the antigens.
> (ironic)
> Pretty soon, he'll be ringing the bell at Notre Dame.

> HARRY
> (frustrated)
> So, what am I s'posed to do, Tully? Get drunk and go bowling?

> WOIWODE
> Business as usual, Harry. . . .

> HARRY
> At least let me talk to Eli—

> WOIWODE
> The General ain't around.

> HARRY
> Then let me join the Friends. I want to do something—

> WOIWODE
> Stay close to the Senator—tell us everything on his sick little mind. You want to be a samurai, Harry? Now's your chance.

EXT. WALT WHITMAN PUBLIC LIBRARY—DAY

ESTABLISHING SHOT of the defunct library, new shelter for the Friends since they decamped the bathhouse.

INT. WALT WHITMAN PUBLIC LIBRARY—GRACE'S ROOM—DAY

Japanese-style; sliding screens and tatami. GRACE lays in bed, bruised from her ordeal. She is depressed, still recovering from her assault. Her father sits beside her, stroking her hair.

> ELI
> How are you?

> GRACE
> Why didn't they just kill me?

> ELI
> Josie must have intervened.

(CONTINUED)

> GRACE
> (smirks)
> If it was up to Josie, I'd be buried somewhere
> under the Hollywood sign.
> (beat)
> I miss my baby.

> ELI
> I know.

> GRACE
> Do you think she's safe?

> ELI
> Yes. We'll get her back.

> GRACE
> (sarcastic)
> Like we got Chickie?
> (beat)
> Why did you take my tapes away?

> ELI
> I don't want you watching them. Torturing
> yourself . . .

> GRACE
> Don't you like seeing your little granddaughter?

> ELI
> It isn't her: It's a trick, Grace! They just want to
> get to you. They dump those tapes on the black
> market—new ones, every few days. . . .

> GRACE
> But what if it isn't a trick?

> ELI
> She talks, Grace! Why would Deirdre suddenly
> talk—on tape, and for strangers? It's not her.

Grace is crying.

> ELI
> I'm sorry. Get some rest now. I love you.

He kisses her, exits. She waits a beat, then takes a cassette that's
been hidden beneath her pillow. She puts it into machine, settles
back.

OUTSIDE SCREEN

Hiro approaches sliding screen, trailed discreetly by Peter. Hiro starts
to enter Grace's room; stops as cassette begins to play.

(CONTINUED)

We see Grace's silhouette projected onto screen; then a smaller silhouette—the holosynth of the little girl. (Deirdre remains unseen—seen only as silhouette, through screen.)

                    DEIRDRE (V.O.)
          Mommy? It's Deirdre.
                    (softly crying)
          I miss you! Why won't you come rescue me?
          They're hurting me, Mommy! Why won't you
          come?

Grace sobs convulsively—her silhouette heaves—and Hiro retreats, embarrassed to be privy to such bizarre and desperate intimacies.

CLOSE ON GRACE

sobbing. Trying not to look at this counterfeit image of her daughter, an image she wants so much to be real. . . .

                                        FADE OUT.

                    END OF ACT ONE

<u>ACT TWO</u>

FADE IN:

EXT. WYCKOFF HOUSE—BACK YARD—NIGHT

Winds blow the palms, rippling the pool's dirty water. The house has fallen a little to seed since Grace has been gone.

INT. WYCKOFF HOUSE—MASTER BEDROOM—NIGHT

Shadows of the trees fall across Harry's face as he sleeps. He winces, as if in pain; still asleep, he scratches one hand with the other. He awakens, scratching some more. He turns on light, looks at hand and gasps.

CLOSE ON HAND

The part with palm tattoo is hideously inflamed.

The WIND blows OPEN a WINDOW, startling him.

INT. MEDICAL BUILDING—DAY—EXAMINING ROOM—DAY

Harry's hand is being bandaged by Dr. Arnold Klein, a wavy-haired physician in his fifties.

                    HARRY
          What was it?

                    DOCTOR KLEIN
          A cyst.
                    (hands him pills)
          I want you to take these for a week.

                    HARRY
          Antibiotics?

                    DOCTOR KLEIN
          You've got an infection. Who gave you the tattoo,
          Harry?

                    HARRY
          Guy on Hollywood Boulevard somewhere—I was
          drunk.

                    DOCTOR KLEIN
          Midlife crisis?

                    HARRY
          Lighten up, will you, Doc?

                    DOCTOR KLEIN
          Do you have an hour? You're due for a physical;
          it's been a couple of years.

                                        (CONTINUED)

> HARRY
> I can't—I have to go to the desert to meet the
> Senator.

> DOCTOR KLEIN
> Are they going to get him on the ballots?

> HARRY
> That's the idea.

He starts to exit.

> DOCTOR KLEIN
> (patting Harry's shoulder)
> By the way, I'm sorry about Grace. Hope it all
> works out.

Harry exits. Dr. Klein immediately gets on the phone. Klein's
underlined dialogue is in subtitled Japanese.

> DOCTOR KLEIN
> It's Klein. He was here—<u>I removed the chip.</u>

EXT. WILD PALMS—DAY

ESTABLISHING SHOT.

INT. WILD PALMS—STUDY—DAY

Harry is led inside by a servant. On TV, the Senator is sitting on a
couch—with TED KOPPEL.

> KOPPEL (V.O.)
> We're talking with Presidential aspirant Senator
> Tony Kreutzer—the man who dragged us, for
> better or for worse, into the age of virtual
> telepresence. Let's talk about Synthiotics—

> SENATOR (V.O.)
> Been talking about it for thirty years, Ted.

> KOPPEL (V.O.)
> One social critic defined the quasi-religious
> movement as, and I quote, "a dangerous cult of
> techno-shamanists whose members worship its
> billionaire founder while proselytizing dark visions
> of brave new realism." Just what are the goals of
> Synthiotics, Senator, and what role will the group
> play if you're elected?

> SENATOR (V.O.)
> Ted, you forgot <u>Time</u> magazine: They called us
> the 'riptide for reality surfers.'

(CONTINUED)

> KOPPEL (V.O.)
> If we could strike an at least tentative agreement
> that you'll answer the questions posed—

> SENATOR (V.O.)
> There's a saying we have at Synthiotics 'What a
> difference an 'A' makes'—with the tiny letter 'a',
> you can change a <u>worrier</u> to a <u>warrior.</u> . . .

> KOPPEL (V.O)
> Let's leapfrog the homilies for a moment, if we
> may—

The Senator enters, LOWERING the VOLUME with the remote until
Koppel is BARELY AUDIBLE.

> SENATOR
> Powerful stuff, don't you think?

> HARRY
> Very effective.

> SENATOR
> After the Koppel show, I jumped eighteen points
> in the polls.

> PAIGE
> (entering)
> Hello, Harry.

> HARRY
> Paige.

> SENATOR
> What happened to your hand?

> HARRY
> A cyst.

> SENATOR
> Come out to the garden, Harry. I want to talk to
> you.
> (to Paige; while exiting)
> Your old boyfriend and I are going to compare
> notes.

> PAIGE
> Very funny.

The Senator exits; Harry follows. Before he can leave the room, Paige
buttonholes him; she's agitated.

> PAIGE
> Something's wrong. . . .

(CONTINUED)

                        HARRY
Tell me—

                        PAIGE
They killed Ushio last night. . . .

                        HARRY
The guy who gave me the tattoo?
                    (she nods)
Where? In Kyoto?

                        PAIGE
No—here in L.A.! In the Wilderzone.

                        HARRY
What's it all about?

                        PAIGE
Harry, I'm scared. . . .

                        HARRY
It's all right.

                        PAIGE
Be careful!

EXT. WILD PALMS—POOL/ZEN GARDEN—DAY

Harry and the Senator beside the pool. They sit down on chaise
lounges; there's a table with fruit, etc. The Senator nibbles.

                        SENATOR
Hungry, Harry?

                        HARRY
No—I grabbed something on the way.

                        SENATOR
Everybody's hungry.
                    (beat)
Everybody's a hungry ghost. . . .

                        HARRY
            (reacts to reference; then, cool)
What do you mean?

                        SENATOR
It's a Buddhist thing, like our Hell—hungry ghosts
are souls doomed to wander the earth in torment
and insatiable desire.

                        HARRY
Should I develop that?

The Senator is nonplussed.

                                              (CONTINUED)

                            HARRY
Sounds like a Channel Three sitcom.

The Senator laughs explosively.

                            SENATOR
Do you play the ponies, Harry?

                            HARRY
Once in awhile. I like the exactas.

                            SENATOR
Santa Anita—lovely track. They used it during the
Second World War. Called it an 'assembly center.'

                            HARRY
For the camps?

                            SENATOR
                            (nods)
Moved 'em out from there: Heart Mountain,
Manzanar . . . people have forgotten all that. Did
you know my father was a preacher, Harry? Met
Mama at a revival, settled on Bunker Hill. That's
where I was born—a stone's throw from Angel's
Flight.
                            (beat)
You could take a trolley to the sea back then. I
still remember it; gallingly blue. Pearl Harbor
changed everything—for Mama.

                            HARRY
                            (puzzled)
Your mother was Japanese?

                            SENATOR
Just a drop—enough to satisfy executive order
9066. They sent her to Manzanar.

                            HARRY
Jesus.

                            SENATOR
He never took us to see her, not once. Crazy-
drunk all the time. Mama was in the desert, he
said, helping government agents bury children
who were bad—so we'd better stay away! She
died a few weeks before the camps were
liberated.

                            HARRY
And your father?

                                            (CONTINUED)

> SENATOR
> Cirrhosis—thank God. I still think of him
> wandering this earth, speaking in tongues . . . the
> original Hungry Ghost.

Suddenly he reaches over and tears off Harry's bandage; the
Senator's demeanor changes from reflective to wild-eyed. Harry
stands; Paige appears nervously in b.g. Rapid-fire:

> HARRY
> What the Hell are you doing?

> SENATOR
> What did they give you in Kyoto?

> HARRY
> What are you talking about?

> SENATOR
> Was it the GO chip, Harry?

> HARRY
> No—

> SENATOR
> Ushio gave it to you, he said so! Why would he
> lie?

> HARRY
> I don't know—

> SENATOR
> Does Woiwode have it?

> HARRY
> I don't know—

> SENATOR
> Would you betray me, Harry?

> HARRY
> No!

> SENATOR
> Would you keep me from eternity? Why did you
> go to the doctor?

> HARRY
> I had a cyst removed—

> SENATOR
> Is that what eternity is? A cyst?

The Senator grabs Harry and kisses him, Godfather-style. The kiss of
death. Men in Suits appear.

(CONTINUED)

SENATOR

My <u>son</u>!

Harry exits, leery and unsteady—thoroughly tweaked. He's expecting
the Men in Suits to come after him, but they don't . . . not yet. He
throws Paige a look as he exits.

EXT. JOSIE'S CONDOMINIUM—DAY

Coty snorkels underwater; surfaces. Standing at edge of pool—in his
face—is Peter. Pete wears his backpack; Coty takes off face mask.

PETER

Looking for someone? It's so much easier if you
drain the pool first.

COTY

The prodigal son returns!

PETER

With a message: <u>Leave Grace alone.</u>

Coty lifts himself out of pool.

COTY
(mocking)

And <u>so</u> demanding.

PETER

Don't you feel anything? She was a mother to
you!

COTY
(toweling off)

There <u>are</u> no mothers—only fathers! And you're
trespassing—

PETER

They're using you, Coty. Soon you'll be too
famous—you'll be dangerous to them. . . .

COTY

You're <u>pathetic</u>—why don't you go sell a map?

PETER

Do you think Josie's going to let you have any
real power?

COTY

You better get outta here—

PETER

She'll have you killed, and no one'll even know.
When the ratings drop, they'll sell your image like
(MORE)

(CONTINUED)

> PETER (CONT'D)
> an old video game. You'll be a relic, a Milton
> Berle. Mr. Virtual Television!

> COTY
> (menacing)
> Little <u>freak</u>! I'll put you in that pool and your dirty
> friends won't be waiting under the drain!

Coty grabs Peter, hauls off and belts him, sending him reeling. Before
Peter can get up, Coty throws himself on him, pummeling. (NOTE:
This fight should be "down and dirty" and indistinguishable from a
classic "grown-up" brawl—the boys should fight with an awesome,
strange precociousness.)

Peter has the upper hand; the squirming Coty is pinned.

> PETER
> <u>Leave my mother alone!</u>

He delivers a final blow, then exits. Coty stands shakily, rubbing his
jaw—the lip bleeds.

> COTY
> (malevolently)
> You're too late, little punk! We made sure she
> was in church early—she's praying right now!

Peter reacts, then turns and bolts.

INT. CHURCH OF SYNTHIOTICS—DAY

Grace enters. She looks around for the subject of her rendezvous.

> GRACE
> Deirdre? Mama's here. I came, baby, just like you
> told me to! Are you here?

Silence.

> GRACE
> Josie? I want to see my baby!

Peter slips in noiselessly. He's out of breath. Grace looks toward
where he's come in, then hears a voice from the other direction,
inside the church:

> DEIRDRE (V.O.)
> Mommy, I miss you!

Grace runs toward the voice—Deirdre stands there, arms
outstretched.

> GRACE
> Baby!

(CONTINUED)

Grace runs to her, throwing arms around her—then crashes "through" her daughter to the floor; Deirdre's holosynth keeps TALKING, on a "loop."

> DEIRDRE (V.O.)
> I miss you! Why won't you come rescue me?
> They're hurting me, Mommy! Why won't you—

ANGLE ON PETER

hidden in a niche. He takes the MimeCam from backpack and begins to film.

ANGLE ON GRACE

While Deirdre (holosynth) REPEATS herself, Grace, still on floor, begins to weep, head hanging down. We HEAR the ECHO of APPROACHING FOOTSTEPS. Grace looks up to see—her mouth and eyes widen with fear.

ANGLE ON GLOVED HAND

pressing STOP on remote control—Deirdre's holosynth vanishes.

CLOSE ON PETER AND MIMECAM

A fat tear rolls down Peter's cheek as he records the oncoming events.

INT. MEDICAL BUILDING—DR. KLEIN'S OFFICE—DAY

Ransacked. CAMERA TRACKS PAST MAN IN SUIT on phone, over littered floor to Klein's desk.

> MAN IN SUIT
> It's not here, Senator. We're too late.

Dr. Arnold Klein sits in chair, neck stretched back, mouth wide open.

CLOSE ON MOUTH

Inside is stuffed a small plastic rhino—like the one belonging to Coty that was found on the body of Gavin Whitehope.

INT. CITY RESTAURANT/WILD PALMS STUDY—NIGHT

INTERCUT Harry and Paige on phones.

We SLOWLY REVEAL that Tobias Schenkl sits close to Paige as she talks, while the Senator stares out a window, musing. The winds blow the palms wildly. It should be obvious that Paige is in a terrible bind—she has to play out the scene without revealing her ties to Harry.

(CONTINUED)

                           HARRY
          Paige? It's me. . . .

                            PAIGE
          Where are you?

                           HARRY
          A restaurant. Listen—

                            PAIGE
          Are you okay?

                           HARRY
          Yeah—sort of . . .

                            PAIGE
          What's going on?

                           HARRY
                 (looks at bandaged hand)
          I can't go home—
                      (laughs)
          —wherever that is! Paige, I think they're gonna
          kill me. . . .

Paige turns away from Tobias, so he can't see a tear zoom down her
cheek.

                            PAIGE
          I'll come get you—

                           HARRY
          No! I'm going down to the Wilderzone. I don't
          know when I'll be able to—

A hand hangs up the phone—LIEUTENANT GRINDROD.

                       LT. GRINDROD
          Hello, Harry.

                           HARRY
          Well, well—old Ma Grindrod. That was rude.

                       LT. GRINDROD
          Don't give me any crap. Let's go. . . .

Harry's grabbed by Men in Suits.

                           HARRY
          Get offa me!

A fight ensues—Harry gets off a few punches, but is overpowered.

                       LT. GRINDROD
          You're under arrest!

                                          (CONTINUED)

                              HARRY
                         (out of breath)
                 For what, you sonofabitch?

Grindrod pads him down, removes gun from Harry's coat pocket.

                         LT. GRINDROD
              The murder of Grace Wyckoff. . . .

They gag him, drag him from restaurant past dining couple who
curiously watch the scene—we HOLD ON them as they coolly go
back to menus. The WAITER ENTERS FRAME.

                              WAITER
              Let me start with the specials: We've got
              mesquite-grilled mahi-mahi, a pasta puttanesca,
              and a paillard of chicken with lemon and dill—

                                                  FADE OUT.

                      END OF ACT TWO

ACT THREE

FADE IN:

INT. RESORT—CORRIDORS—NIGHT

Harry, gagged, heavily restrained—and now blindfolded—thrashes as he's wheeled on gurney through corridor. The gurney crashes through doors marked: THE PHARM.

INFIRMARY

Harry's eyes widen with hope when he sees Tobias Schenkl. Tobias removes his gag as several Attendants retreat to b.g. (NOTE: following should be played with machine-gun speed.)

> HARRY
> Tobias! Where am I?

> TOBIAS
> The Perceptory. I don't know where the order came from—

> HARRY
> Grindrod . . . I thought he was going to kill me!
> He said Grace was—

> TOBIAS
> She's dead.

> HARRY
> Oh God! Tobias, they killed her!

> TOBIAS
> You're in trouble, Harry! Where did you get the gun?

> HARRY
> What gun?!

> TOBIAS
> It's the same that killed Mazie Woiwode—

> HARRY
> They set me up! The Senator's insane—he killed
> Grace! He's holding my daughter!

> TOBIAS
> Listen, Harry, you've got to tell them everything—

> HARRY
> (confused)
> Everything . . .

(CONTINUED)

> TOBIAS
> You don't know what you're up against!

> HARRY
> Someone's gotta get to Tommy! Gotta warn
> them—

> TOBIAS
> He doesn't <u>care</u> about them. He only wants the
> chip. Where is it, Harry? Tell them or you'll never
> get out of here!

> HARRY
> Tobias, I don't know!

> TOBIAS
> (turns to Nurse; cold)
> <u>Mimezine—a thousand units.</u>

Harry's in shock at Tobias' betrayal. He screams; as Tobias talks, they
gag him again. The Nurse quickly injects him, as Tobias pulls a pair
of eiglasses from his pocket.

> TOBIAS
> I scream, you scream—we all scream for ice
> cream . . .

He gently slides them onto Harry's face.

INT. WYCKOFF HOUSE—KITCHEN—DAY

Harry enters tentatively as Grace works the cappuccino
machine—we've come full circle again. Grace walks to banquette,
pouring him a cup. He stands there gaping at her—she blushes.

> GRACE
> What's the matter?

> HARRY
> They . . . they told me you died.

> GRACE
> (smiling)
> Have you been having one of your crazy dreams?

He notices a spot of blood near her heart.

> HARRY
> What's that?

> GRACE
> Just a flesh wound. How do you want your eggs?

Harry sits in banquette, unable to assess what's happening to him.
Grace sits down beside him, solicitous.

(CONTINUED)

>   HARRY
>   (smiles strangely)
> Something's weird—what is it, Grace? What's the
> matter with me?

>   GRACE
> Working too hard, I guess.
>   (kisses him)
> Love me?

>   HARRY
>   (connecting for the first time)
> Yes . . .
>   (emotional)
> I'm so sorry, Grace—about everything that's
> happened. Maybe we can start over.

>   GRACE
> We can! Once you tell them where they can find
> the GO chip, we'll leave this place forever.

Harry's confused by what she says.

>   COTY (O.S.)
> Daddy, come look!

He stands, exits. Grace stops him as he goes out door.

>   GRACE
> Don't forget your briefcase.

She hands him a samurai sword. He takes it from her; slips it into
sheath on his side.

EXT. WYCKOFF HOUSE—BACK YARD—DAY

The palms shimmy in the wind. Harry emerges from house.

>   HARRY
> Coty?

Coty is nowhere to be seen. As if compelled, Harry descends stairs
into basin. He's focussed on drain at deep end. By the time Harry
reaches drain, there's a foot or two of water. He tugs at trapdoor-
drain, trying to pull it off; it won't budge. Grace exits onto patio; she
is bleeding more now.

>   GRACE
> You've got to break with Tommy and
> Tully—they're the ones who got you into all of
> this! I'd never have been killed if it wasn't for
> those terrible men! You've got to tell the Senator
> what you know about the GO chip—

> HARRY
> I already told them, Grace—I don't know
> anything!

Harry still tugs at trapdoor-drain, but water's approaching chin-level.

> GRACE
> Do you know what it's like to be shot, Harry?
> Don't you even love us? You care more about a
> bunch of terrorists than you do your own flesh
> and blood!

Suddenly, the trapdoor opens—a hand grabs Harry's ankle. He panics as the water rises over his head.

UNDERWATER. The man holding Harry's ankle emerges from drain. It's Dex, Harry's father. His T-shirt reads, DEX WYCKOFF b. 1943 d. 1972—"Father and Friend." Dex manages to speak with absolute clarity:

> DEX WYCKOFF
> Tell them what you know, Harry! Tell them or
> you won't wake up!

Harry opens his mouth in horror and the water rushes in. . . .

INT. RESORT—INFIRMARY—DAY

Harry screams as one of the ATTENDANTS removes "eiglasses."

> NURSE (ATTENDANT)
> He's going into shock!

> TOBIAS
> (cool)
> He doesn't know anything; he would have talked.
> Give him the antigen—then get him the Hell outta
> here.

CLOSE ON Harry, eyes opened—horror and deep tremors.

EXT. WALT WHITMAN PUBLIC LIBRARY—DAY

ESTABLISHING SHOT.

INT. WALT WHITMAN PUBLIC LIBRARY—COMMUNAL AREA—DAY

The incongruously elegant interior: Japanese screens and vases of orchids. ELI, TULLY and HIRO sit in darkness.

> ELI
> How's the boy?

(CONTINUED)

HIRO

He won't eat.

WOIWODE

Won't talk either.

HIRO

They charged Harry with Grace's murder. He's at
the Resort.

ELI

I thought he was our salvation—he turns out to be
weak. Tully—could I have been so wrong . . .
about everything?

WOIWODE

I stopped looking for answers a long time ago, Eli.
It's all like bad haiku.

ELI

I want a War Meeting—at MacArthur Park. Put
that out on the street. Where's Tommy?

HIRO

At the bazaar—the black market stalls.

ELI

Mimezine? He's gotta stop using it; we have to get
him to Dr. Klein. Hiro—pick him up.

WOIWODE

I know where to find him.

Hiro and Woiwode exit.

EXT. WILDERZONE—BAZAAR—DAY

A wasted-looking Tommy among the smoke and clamor of the stalls:
a throng of gawkers and illicit traders, where black marketeers
comingle with shadowy hawkers of roasted animals on sticks,
erotica/exotica, wholesale high-tech goodies and illegal
unmentionables. Tommy fights his way against the current until he
reaches the PURVEYOR—an ageless decadent in dreadlocks.

PURVEYOR

Hey, Dream Boy! Back for more?

TOMMY

I only have enough for a gram. . . .

PURVEYOR

Whatchoo <u>doin'</u> with the stuff, Dream Boy? Can't
be taking it all yourself—

(CONTINUED)

> TOMMY
> (acerbic)
> It's for my mother.

Tommy hands her cash, but Purveyor withholds the tiny lidded cup of Mimezine for a beat as she hawks her wares.

> PURVEYOR
> How 'bout some holotapes to get you through the night?
> (looks through cassettes)
> Got some travel tapes . . . some sex stuff—very hot. How 'bout Casablanca—play it again, Dream Boy!

> TOMMY
> Just gimme the Mimezine!

> PURVEYOR
> (hands it to him)
> You're one 'gimme-gimme,' Dream Boy.
> (after him)
> You know where to find me!

We TRACK Tommy as he leaves bazaar. Suddenly, blue fluid from his nose and the DEAFENING RING of CHURCH BELLS (that no one else can hear). He reels from street, to back alley, hands over ears in agony.

TOMMY'S POV

He cowers beside imaginary cathedral (CF. END OF 4TH HOUR).

BACK TO SCENE

He manages to take the lid off the cup of Mimezine and swig it down. He waits for RINGING to subside.

EXT. MARINA—YACHT—DAY

A chauffeured limousine pulls up to The Floating World, stops. Men in blazers guard gangway, deck.

PROW

Josie lays on chaise lounge, holding silver sun-screen to her face. Coty, impeccably dressed in a Synthiotics maritime-style uniform, approaches from aft.

> JOSIE
> Ahoy, Captain. Don't you look grand.

> COTY
> Deirdre's been cooped up too long—it isn't healthy.

(CONTINUED)

                              JOSIE
Has she complained?
                              (ironic)
I haven't heard a word.

                              COTY
                    (sits beside her; pensive)
Grandma . . . what's going to happen after
'Church Windows'? You know—when people get
tired of watching.

                              JOSIE
They'll <u>never</u> get tired—

                              COTY
Don't lie to me. In a year, I could be history.

                              JOSIE
                           (smiles)
What's got into you?

                              COTY
Are there other shows being developed?

                              JOSIE
Of course there are.

                              COTY
For me?

                              JOSIE
Yes. Don't be silly!

                              COTY
What are they?

                              JOSIE
                       (back to sunning)
Well, I don't know, darling. That's the
programmers' domain . . .

                              COTY
I want the details—<u>now.</u>

                              JOSIE
You're acting like a child—

He grabs the sun-screen, using it to roughly slap her face; leans
menacingly forward.

                              COTY
Don't <u>ever</u> say that! And don't you underestimate
me! When you killed your daughter, your pulse
never rose above normal—we're alike that way.
                           (MORE)

                                                            (CONTINUED)

> COTY (CONT'D)
> But my crimes will be grander, I assure you: One
> day, I'll put out the sun—and make bare every
> womb there ever was.

EXT. WILD PALMS—NIGHT

ESTABLISHING SHOT.

INT. WILD PALMS—TERRACE/LIVING ROOM—NIGHT

SINATRA (or STARFALL) on the STEREO. The Senator is looking
through the telescope at the stars. He wears one of his grandiose silk
robes. He walks to living room, where Paige sits on floor, smoking;
she drinks from a large snifter while doing jigsaw puzzle—an all-
black one, like Grace's.

> SENATOR
> I had the dream again—the buried children.

> PAIGE
> There's too much pressure. Why don't you drop
> the campaign?

> SENATOR
> Fix me a drink, will you?
>   (she stands; goes to wet-bar)
> Tobias really botched it with Harry.

> PAIGE
> What happened?

> SENATOR
> Just when he was going to tell us all about the
> GO chip, Harry had a big, old, scary heart attack.

He impishly watches Paige's reaction.

> SENATOR
> Just kidding—but, very good! You hardly flinched!
> (as Paige abruptly stands, exits; he goes after her)
> Where are you going?

> PAIGE
> (angry)
> I think I'll sleep in town tonight—in my own
> bed—

> SENATOR
> (grabs her arm)
> Oh, no you're not. You're going for a drive—I
> want you to pick up Harry at the Resort and take
> him to the Wilderzone.

(CONTINUED)

PAIGE
How—?

SENATOR
In half an hour, Channel Three will announce that
the arrest of attorney Harry Wyckoff was an error;
police have picked up the real killer—in Toshiba
Park.

PAIGE
I don't understand—

SENATOR
I need him <u>out</u> of jail—we made a deal with
someone. . . .

PAIGE
How can I take Harry <u>anywhere</u>? I'm known; I'll
be recognized.

SENATOR
Not in the Wilderzone.

PAIGE
What am I supposed to do?

SENATOR
Eli has the GO chip. If I go after him in force,
he'll destroy it out of sheer spite. I want you to set
up an exchange: the chip—for Deirdre.

EXT. CHANNEL THREE—NIGHT

The street in front of the network has been cleared. About a dozen
unmarked police cars with revolving red lights stuck onto roofs.

Lieutenant Grindrod and Tobias Schenkl sit in the back of unmarked
sedan. The air is tense—Grindrod champs at the bit.

LIEUTENANT GRINDROD
Let's take him—<u>now.</u>

TOBIAS
No! He said nine-thirty—he'll come. Remember:
This was <u>his</u> idea.

LIEUTENANT GRINDROD
That's what bothers me. Has to be one of Levitt's
tricks—

TOBIAS
He'll <u>be</u> here. He's making the supreme sacrifice
for his first love—<u>very</u> Japanese.
(looks O.S.)
There he is . . .

(CONTINUED)

Grindrod and Tobias exit car while police stiffen in combat stance, weapon-ready.

A figure stands a few dramatic beats in the shadows, then steps into light: It's Hiro. The <u>underlined</u> is in Japanese:

> HIRO
> (to self; sotto)
> It's better this way, Grace—Harry will be with the children. <u>And I will be with you . . . my love.</u>

He smiles abstractly, begins to laugh. Then, loudly:

> HIRO
> Beat me up, Scotty!

The police descend.

EXT. RESORT—NIGHT

Harry and Paige tear out in Corvette, speeding onto dark ribbon of highway. Paige at the wheel; Harry shivers.

> PAIGE
> Are you all right?

She grabs blanket from backseat, pushing it on him. He mutters, seemingly delirious.

> PAIGE
> Here—cover yourself.

> HARRY
> (muttering)
> Bring 'em, Paige . . . Paige? Bring em . . . bring—

> PAIGE
> What? Harry—?

> HARRY
> . . . gonna bring em, Paige—bring 'em . . .
> I'm—bring—

A slow, purposeful smile spreads across his face as Paige looks over, trying to understand. Harry's eyes are clear, hard, resolute—almost serene.

> HARRY
> <u>I'm gonna bring 'em down.</u>

They rocket past row of swirling palms.

We STAY ON PALMS as we:

FADE OUT.

<u>END OF ACT THREE</u>

ACT FOUR

FADE IN:

INT. WALT WHITMAN PUBLIC LIBRARY—TOMMY'S ROOM/ COMMUNAL AREA—DAY

Tommy shivers, laid out on a futon, in one of the spare, Japanese-style rooms; Eli tucks a blanket around him. Harry and Paige sit on tatami in half-darkness. He proffers a box; Harry takes it.

> TOMMY
> For you, old friend . . .

Harry opens the box: a menacing dagger is within—the shape of a rhino horn. Eli Levitt nods at Harry and Paige to exit. They walk around screen to communal area.

> HARRY
> Is there any way to help him?

> ELI
> (shakes his head)
> His system's been <u>pickled</u> in Mimezine; got too much of it in jail—a thousand units all at once . . .

Precisely what happened to Harry; Harry and Paige exchange looks.

> ELI
> I gave him something. He'll sleep.

Eli pours them tea. Harry and Paige follow.

> ELI
> The Senator's already made the ballots in sixty-three of the states. He's going to announce his running mate tonight, right after 'Church Windows'—who will that be, Paige?

> PAIGE
> Josie.

> ELI
> Perfect.

> HARRY
> (to Eli)
> Do you have a plan?

> ELI
> I've set a War Meeting—I'll suggest we blow Channel Three all the way to hell.

(CONTINUED)

                        HARRY
What will that do, Eli?

                         ELI
Put a serious crimp in Sweeps Week . . .

                        HARRY
The public'll turn on you. Besides, it'll barely slow
them down; I <u>know</u>—I worked there, remember?

                         ELI
                      (intense)
Channel Three is the beating heart of Wild
Palms—

                        HARRY
You've been in prison too long! They have too
many arms. . . .

                        PAIGE
Eli, he's right—

                         ELI
                     (to Paige)
<u>You</u> stay out of this!

                        HARRY
Even if you did some damage, they'd reroute and
broadcast from the compound in the desert.

                         ELI
That will be our second target.

                        HARRY
<u>Be subtle, to the point of formlessness</u> . . .

                         ELI
A little poetry, Harry?

                        HARRY
Sun Tzu—<u>The Art of War.</u>

                         ELI
                      (biting)
Bravo! Harry Wyckoff—television executive and
weekend warrior!

                        HARRY
<u>Be mysterious, to the point of soundlessness</u> . . .

                         ELI
No more quotes! They took my children from me!

                        HARRY
From <u>all</u> of us!

(CONTINUED)

                              PAIGE
                          (after a beat)
            The Senator wants a trade—Deirdre, for the GO
            chip.

                               ELI
            Once he has the chip, we'll have nothing left. No
            game.

An aide enters, whispers in Eli's ear; bows, exits.

                             HARRY
            We go against him with arms—we lose. There has
            to be another way. . . .

                               ELI
            The boy wants to see you.

                             HARRY
            The boy?

                               ELI
            Peter.

GRACE'S ROOM

Harry enters. Peter turns in the bed, sees him; throws his arms
around him in desperation. Harry's flustered. Peter is crying.

                             HARRY
            It's all right! It's all right, little man.

                             PETER
            Don't go! Don't leave me, Daddy!

                             HARRY
                      (confused by "Daddy")
            I won't. I'm here—

                             PETER
            Did they tell you I was there when Grace died?

                             HARRY
            They told me.

                             PETER
            I saw her killed! I could have saved her! But I
            couldn't move—when it started, I couldn't move!

Peter cries.

                             HARRY
            Don't, Peter—

                                PETER
                After they left, I went to her. We talked. She knew
                who I was—I <u>know</u> she did! She called me her
                'wild child.' Then she—

                                HARRY
                                (fishing)
                —'Knew' who you were?

                                PETER
                My foster parents always told me I was switched
                with another baby boy—they made it a joke, but
                it wasn't!
                                (cries again)
                Why did they have to kill her?

                                HARRY
                It's all right now . . .

He reaches under his pillow for the cassette.

                                PETER
                I want you to have it.

                                HARRY
                                (takes it)
                What is it?

                                PETER
                I want to go home! Please, Daddy! Take me
                home!

Harry rocks the boy in his arms, and stares at holocassette-recording
of Grace's murder.

INT. METROPOLITAN DETENTION CENTER—DAY

An INMATE holds mirror through bars to see adjacent cell.

                                INMATE
                Hiro!

In adjacent cell, Hiro does the same.

                                HIRO
                What's happening?

                                INMATE
                Grapevine says you're being transferred to the
                Resort.

                                HIRO
                When?

(CONTINUED)

> INMATE
> Sometime tonight. Beware the Pharm, man! They
> play with your head. . . .

> HIRO
> Don't worry, Chico. I come from a long line of
> tough bastards—my grandpa liberated Dachau!
> Let them come.

> INMATE
> <u>Deru kugi wa utareru.</u>
>   SUBTITLE: The nail that sticks up gets
>   pounded down!
> Ciao, baby.

Hiro retreats to his cell. A small television flickers in the ceiling
corner. He lifts his mattress. From underneath, he removes a silken
sack; sits on floor, empties it. Inside are the old black-and-white
photo of him and Grace, a red kerchief, and a "shank" made from a
spoon, with masking tape around handle. He ties kerchief around his
head and sets photo down before him. Then Hiro takes the shank
and aims it inward, toward his stomach.

CAMERA PANS OFF him TO television.

> ANCHORMAN (V.O.)
> (on TV)
> . . . amidst a storm of speculation, Independent
> presidential candidate Senator Tony Kreutzer will
> announce his running mate tonight from Wild
> Palms, his desert home. An A.B.C. News poll
> showed the Senator would garner sixty-two
> percent of the vote in the three-way race with
> incumbent . . .

INT. CHANNEL THREE—ENTRANCE ATRIUM—NIGHT

Harry waves to puzzled NIGHTMAN, who unlocks the glass door.

> STEVE THE NIGHTMAN
> Mr. Wyckoff?

> HARRY
> Hiya, Steve! Sorry to bust in on you like this—left
> some papers in my office—

> STEVE THE NIGHTMAN
> (confused)
> I didn't think you <u>had</u> an office anymore . . .

> HARRY
> Don't you read the papers? They let me outta jail!

> STEVE THE NIGHTMAN
> I know that, but—

(CONTINUED)

                    HARRY
It'll just take a second. . . .

                STEVE THE NIGHTMAN
Where's your access card?

                    HARRY
                  (laughs)
Demagnetized—my son threw it in the pool—

                STEVE THE NIGHTMAN
I can't let you in, Mr. Wyckoff.

                    HARRY
Okay. No problem. How 'bout letting me use the
can?

Steve firmly shakes his head; Harry laughs, casually.

                    HARRY
                  (comical)
Steve, you're killing me!

With unexpected speed, Harry punches Steve out, drags him behind
atrium desk, exits into building.

INT. WILD PALMS—STUDY—NIGHT

The Senator and Paige talk by the bar. In b.g., Josie and Coty sit on
couch, waiting for SHOW to BEGIN—the "Church Windows" title
suddenly appears in middle of room, accompanied by THEME.

                    PAIGE
Harry and I met with Eli in the Zone. He has the
chip; he'll make the exchange. He just needs a
little time.

                    SENATOR
Thank you, darling . . .

Paige and the Senator join Coty and Josie. Tabba's Holo appears,
along with pews and stained glass. She stands at easel, painting;
wears an absurd beret and artist's smock.

                COTY'S CHARACTER (V.O.)
                  (on TV)
Ma?

                TABBA'S CHARACTER (V.O.)
                  (on TV)
Down here, honey!

**INT. WALT WHITMAN PUBLIC LIBRARY—COMMUNAL
AREA—NIGHT**

                                        (CONTINUED)

Peter and Eli watch the SHOW. THROUGH FOLLOWING, we SLOWLY PAN TO trembling Tommy, in Tully's Woiwode's arms—clearly dying.

> COTY'S CHARACTER (V.O.)
> (on TV)
> I have a confession: I took your false eyelashes.

> TABBA'S CHARACTER (V.O.)
> (on TV; aghast)
> My baby's a cross-dresser!

Canned laughter ON TV.

> COTY'S CHARACTER (V.O.)
> (on TV)
> I used 'em for a science project—

We CUT AWAY.

INT. CHANNEL THREE—CONTROL ROOM—NIGHT

Harry nods at various technicians as he coolly makes his way to inner sanctum of control room, where he confronts ENGINEER.

> HARRY
> Hi.

> ENGINEER
> Who are you?

> HARRY
> Harry Wyckoff.
> (hands him cassette)
> I want you to put this on live feed.

> ENGINEER
> You crazy?

> HARRY
> ("rhino" dagger to his throat)
> Yeah. Now, do it.

INT. WILD PALMS—STUDY/LIVING ROOM—NIGHT

Harry, Paige, Josie and Coty all watch.

> TABBA'S CHARACTER (V.O.)
> (on TV)
> Maybe you're just not cut out to be a scientist.
> Maybe you'll be a statesman, or a writer, or a great painter.

> COTY
> Yeah: house painter.

(CONTINUED)

Laughter in room.

INT. WALT WHITMAN PUBLIC LIBRARY—CLOSE ON TOMMY—NIGHT

He's worse. We hear CHURCH BELLS BEGIN. Woiwode rocks him in his arms. (THROUGHOUT rest of act, SCENES are ACCOMPANIED BY CHURCH BELLS; they begin soft and rhythmic, slowly crescendoing.)

> TOMMY
> Tully? I can hear them! I can hear the bells!

INT. CHANNEL THREE—CONTROL ROOM—NIGHT

The Engineer's fingers are poised over keyboard; Harry presses dagger to his throat.

> HARRY
> Do it.

The Engineer punches in numbers and the tapes begin to roll. Harry brains him with butt of dagger, calmly exits.

INT. WALT WHITMAN PUBLIC LIBRARY—COMMUNAL AREA—NIGHT

In the midst of Tabba and Coty's "Church Windows" characters, Grace (HOLO) appears, kneeling as she did on the day of her death—captured by Peter and the MimeCam. Then Josie (HOLO) enters.

ANGLE ON ELI

He shuts Peter's eyes with his hand so he can't see; draws him near.

> WOIWODE
> Harry did it! Tommy, can you see? Now all the
> world will know—

Tommy, bleeding blue from his nose, smiles weakly.

INT. WILD PALMS—STUDY—NIGHT

Shock and dismay. Josie stands, as if she's seeing ghosts—she is.

> JOSIE'S HOLO
> Get up, dog! Weak dog! When I think I gave birth
> to you, I am seized by revulsion!

> GRACE'S HOLO
> You tricked me! Why, Mother?

(CONTINUED)

> JOSIE'S HOLO
> I used to think you were like your father, but now
> I know: you're not 'like' him—you <u>are</u> him! Now,
> get up!

She pulls Grace up by the hair; Grace screams in pain.

> GRACE'S HOLO
> Mother, please! I want to see my daughter! I'm
> begging you! Let me see my baby!

> JOSIE'S HOLO
> You'll see her—in Hell!

Josie begins to strangle Grace.

INT. WALT WHITMAN PUBLIC LIBRARY—COMMUNAL AREA—NIGHT

Still covering Peter's eyes and holding the boy even closer to him, Eli Levitt weeps as he steals looks at the nightmarish scene before them: the killing of Grace.

Woiwode holds the dead Tommy in his arms. Woiwode weeps, yet is strangely exultant.

> WOIWODE
> Don't leave me now, Tommy! Don't leave me!

The BELLS are almost DEAFENING now. . . .

INT. WILD PALMS—STUDY—CLOSE ON JOSIE—NIGHT

as she screams, in horror.

> JOSIE
> <u>Turn it offffffffffffffff</u>—

EXT. SUBURBAN HOUSES—NIGHT

The RINGING of the BELLS CONTINUES as we TRACK PAST row of houses—the macabre illumination of each living room plays out the killing of Grace at the hands of her mother.

EXT. CHANNEL THREE/STREETS—NIGHT

Harry BURNS RUBBER. Guards exit after him—too late.

INT. CORVETTE—NIGHT

He throws dagger out CAR as he ROCKETS into the night.

(CONTINUED)

>   HARRY
>   (emotional)
>   I'm sorry, Grace! I loved you so! I always will!
>   Good-bye, baby! Good-bye! Good-bye! Good-
>   bye—

The car is sucked up by darkness as we:

                                            FADE OUT.

                        THE END

WILD PALMS

Sixth Hour

"Hello, I Must Be Going"

ACT ONE

FADE IN:

EXT. ELECTION HEADQUARTERS—DAY

Giant posters of the Senator and Josie: KREUTZER 2008! A Range Rover is parked out front. A battered Sixties car ENTERS FRAME. A GIRL gets out, holding a brick.

> GIRL
> This is for Grace Wyckoff!

She hurls the brick through GLASS, SHATTERING it. SCREAMS from inside as people duck for cover. A guy from the car throws something under the Range Rover; the CAR ROARS OFF. After a beat, the Ranger Rover EXPLODES in flames.

INT. WALT WHITMAN PUBLIC LIBRARY—DAY

A war meeting's in progress. A long, oval table. ELI, WOIWODE, HARRY and other FRIENDS and radicals are seated. Harry looks awkward, uncomfortable. The gathered Friends intone a communal prayer (Harry does not join them):

> FRIENDS
> O Captain! My Captain! Our fearful trip is done, the ship has weather'd every rack, the prize we sought is won . . .

> ELI
> Before we begin, I very much want to acknowledge the efforts of one among us: Harry Wyckoff.

The Friends applaud—then rise—to honor him. Harry smiles weakly.

INT. ANOTHER PART OF THE LIBRARY—LATER THAT DAY

The meeting has ended. Harry sits on tatami mat. Eli enters.

> ELI
> How does it feel to be a leader, Harry?

> HARRY
> Viva Zapata. Wanna know how I really feel? Sick! Violated . . . like I killed Grace a second time—on television.

(CONTINUED)

ELI

It got results.

HARRY
(sardonic)
Know what, Eli? They should have moved you
right from the Perceptory to Channel Three—you
would've made a helluva programmer.

ELI
It was a terrible thing, Harry, but it opened
people's eyes—Grace would have demanded that.

HARRY
(caustic)
Don't tell me what she would have
'demanded'—you don't know anything about her!

ELI
What do you want from me?

HARRY
Deirdre. Kreutzer said he would give her to
me—if we gave him the GO chip.

ELI
Can't do it, Harry—

HARRY
(grabbing him roughly)
Why?

ELI
Because with the GO chip, he will become
immortal, a holographic vampire—unstoppable!
From an unspeakable, unreachable place, he will
orchestrate the death of the world—

HARRY
(exiting)
You're crazy as he is!

ELI
Harry, listen—

HARRY
(exits)
I'll have my family back—one way or another. Do
you understand, Eli? Those are my politics.
(beat)
And you can go to Hell.

Harry storms out; Eli slumps down sadly, hand to his face.

INT. WILD PALMS—MASTER BEDROOM—CLOSE ON TV—DAY

(CONTINUED)

Groucho Marx, in <u>Animal Crackers.</u> He sings, "Hello, I Must Be Going." We PAN TO the SENATOR, in bed. A PHYSICIAN takes his blood pressure.

> SENATOR
> Well, what is it, Doc? A heart attack—or indigestion?

> PHYSICIAN
> Stress of the last few days—you're acutely hypertensed. I'd like to put you in Cedars. . . .

> SENATOR
> No hospitals!

> PHYSICIAN
> I can't force you. I'm going to medicate you; I want you in bed—no alcohol or Mimezine . . .

> SENATOR
> You're no fun.
> > (calls out)
> Grindrod!
> > (to Physician)
> What about the GO chip?

> PHYSICIAN
> <u>If</u> I can get your pressure under control, you've got a week or so—after that, I can't say what your body will tolerate. . . .

> SENATOR
> A week, huh . . .
> > (calls out)
> Grindrod!

Lt. Grindrod enters, with Coty behind him, as the Physician exits.

> SENATOR
> Why haven't you bailed Josie?

> LT. GRINDROD
> We're trying—

> SENATOR
> My sister, in <u>jail</u>? What's the <u>matter</u> with you? Get her out—if you have to <u>break</u> her out!

Grindrod exits.

> COTY
> We'll never contain this, Papa—it's a fiasco.

> SENATOR
> Where's the murder tape?

                              COTY
            Being treated at the lab. Even the diehard New
            Realists think Josie's guilty. They're running
            scared—

                              SENATOR
            Then straighten 'em out!

The Senator exits from bed, testily.

EXT. WILD PALMS—TERRACE/ZEN GARDEN—DAY

PAIGE sits on chaise, smoking a cigarette; she looks nervous. The
Senator enters from house, comes close to her.

                              SENATOR
            You knew Harry was going to bust into Channel
            Three, didn't you?

                              PAIGE
            No!

                              SENATOR
            —knew he was going to use that tape! Why,
            Paige?
                         (caressing her hair)
            Am I a handsome man? Am I a virile man?
                         (pulls on hair)
            Answer me!

                              PAIGE
            Tony, please!

                              SENATOR
            Am I a decrepit cuckold?

He grabs her arm, twisting it.

                              PAIGE
            Stop it!

                              SENATOR
            You were supposed to come back with the GO
            chip, but instead you brought a plague to my
            house. . . .

                              PAIGE
            You're hurting me—

                              SENATOR
                         (singing weirdly into her ear)
            'Hello, I must be going! I cannot stay, I came to
            say, I must be going'—

                                                    (CONTINUED)

He throws her down; picks up GLASS table and hurls it to ground, SHATTERING it. Paige cowers as he strides into Zen garden. He lifts one of the heavy stones as he speaks, hurling it into pool. Then he strides through the garden, causing general damage.

> SENATOR
> I assure you: I have not come all this way to die like a trapped wolf, like a circus dog! I am a soldier! I am mustering my troops . . . <u>and we are storming heaven!</u>

EXT. WYCKOFF HOUSE—DAY

Harry drives along in filthy Corvette—by now, it looks like something you'd find in a Wilderzone used car lot. Frustrated and disconsolate, Harry finds himself back at the old house. He exits car, stands in walkway. The place is boarded up; a sad vestige of what it once was. There is graffiti scrawl (some in Japanese): "PRAY FOR THE STOLEN CHILDREN," "REVOLUTION NO. 9," and "WE LOVE YOU, GRACE," etc. Harry walks toward house, feeling the full weight of his journey.

INT. WYCKOFF HOUSE—ENTRYWAY—DAY

Harry enters the ghostly house. More graffiti and litter inside. Some furniture remains; much has been looted.

> HARRY
> (softly)
> Honey? I'm home!

He hears something—from upstairs. Harry grabs a heavy candleholder, ascends stairs.

UPSTAIRS HALL/COTY'S ROOM/DEIRDRE'S ROOM

More noise; DRAWERS OPENING and CLOSING. Harry moves cautiously down hall. The noise emanates from Coty's room.

Harry peers in, ready to strike—PETER'S there, looking through bureau.

> PETER
> Coty's room—I always wanted to see it. It would have been mine. . . .

> HARRY
> Peter, help me out: Why did the Fathers take you from Grace and me? What do you know?

> PETER
> They steal children . . . dreams . . . memories—a regular fire sale. When they say 'everything must go,' they aren't kidding.

(CONTINUED)

HARRY
Why me, Peter? Why my family—

PETER
You really don't know, do you?
(beat)
Let's talk to the source. . . .

HARRY
Wild Palms?

PETER
(nods, ironic)
Should we take the car or the pool?

They smile; Peter takes his hand, leading him out.

EXT. METROPOLITAN DETENTION CENTER—DAY

The PRESS (REPORTERS) await. JOSIE exits building and descends steps, flanked by ATTORNEY and Men in Suits.

REPORTER #1   REPORTER #2
Why'd you kill her, Josie?   How'd you
                               make bail?

JOSIE
I didn't kill anyone.

ATTORNEY
That was a doctored tape—a fabrication—in a few days, we'll prove it!

REPORTER #2   REPORTER #3
Is your brother going to   Will he drop out
choose a new running mate?   of the campaign?

JOSIE
Absolutely not! Why should he?

REPORTER #3
What's your defense going to be?

ATTORNEY
Not guilty!

REPORTER #1
But the whole country saw you murder your daughter.

REPORTER #3
Seeing is believing—

(CONTINUED)

                              JOSIE
                    (to Reporter #3; withering)
              You must be kidding.

She enters limo—Range Rover follows.

INT. LIMO—DAY

Lt. Grindrod and TOBIAS SCHENKL face Josie on opposite fold-out
chairs.

                              JOSIE
              When will the tape be ready?

                         LT. GRINDROD
              Tonight.

                              JOSIE
              And the GO chip?

                         LT. GRINDROD
              I'm assuming Harry Wyckoff is in possession.

                              JOSIE
              Get word out in the Wilderzone: If he doesn't turn
              it over within forty-eight hours, we'll kill the little
              girl.

EXT. WILD PALMS—ZEN GARDEN/POOL—NIGHT

Harry and Peter emerge from bushes, and make their way through
darkness of Zen garden to pool area. Gathered at table around pool
are: the Senator, Paige, Schenkl and Tabba.

Josie enters frame and sits beside Tobias.

                             HARRY
                         (re: Josie)
              They got her out! But how?

ANGLE ON TABLE

Paige looks particularly depressed—the Senator is grim. Josie enters,
takes a seat beside the Senator.

                            SENATOR
              When are we releasing the tape?

                             TOBIAS
              Tomorrow morning: CNN—all the networks.
              Channel Three will run it round the clock.

                              JOSIE
              Eat something. You look haggard.

                                              (CONTINUED)

                              TABBA
                            (to Paige)
          Do you think I should do a feature during hiatus?

                             SENATOR
          What about 'co-conspirators'?

                              TOBIAS
           A Channel Three engineer and two high-level
           MimeCom employees have surrendered
           themselves to state's attorney—New Realist
           Loyalists. They'll admit to eyewitnessing the
           murder and doctoring the tape per Harry
           Wyckoff's orders.

                             SENATOR
          Make sure their families are taken care of.

Coty and DEIRDRE enter—Deirdre goes to Tabba, Coty throws his
arms around the Senator's neck.

                              COTY
          Daddy, can we see it? Can we?

ANGLE ON HARRY AND PETER

Harry's startled to see his baby girl.

                             HARRY
          Deirdre!

Harry makes a move toward her; Peter holds him back.

                             PETER
          Stay back!

BACK TO THE TABLE

Tabba and Deirdre exit as Coty squeals with excitement. The Senator
dims the lights; the tape begins.

BACK TO HARRY

CAMERA PUSHES IN ON Harry—he reacts in stunned horror.

                             HARRY
          My God . . .

ANGLE ON HOLOGRAMS

The Grace/Josie murder tape begins, with the action starting at Grace
kneeling. CAMERA PANS UP, revealing Harry in Josie's place.
Though their words are different, their actions—including the
strangulation—are virtually the same.

                                                    (CONTINUED)

GRACE (V.O.)
Please don't hit me, Harry!

HARRY (V.O.)
You're just like your mother. Now, get up!

BACK TO HARRY AND PETER

Peter pulls at his father, who's riveted by the display.

PETER
Don't look. Don't look!

BACK TO HOLOGRAMS

GRACE (V.O.)
What are you going to do?

HARRY (V.O.)
The Fathers have got to be stopped—I know
you're one of them!

GRACE (V.O.)
No—I'm just a woman! But the Fathers are good,
Harry! They want to bring freedom of images to
the People—

HARRY (V.O.)
As leader of the Friends, I must set the
example—you must die!

GRACE (V.O.)
Please, Harry! Don't hurt me!

HARRY (V.O.)
Long live the Friends! Death to New Realism!
Long live the revolution!

Harry strangles Grace until she dies.

FADE OUT.

END OF ACT ONE

<u>ACT TWO</u>

FADE IN:

EXT. WILDERZONE—BAZAAR—DAY

Woiwode passes through area. The Purveyor emerges from damp black tent set up between stalls.

>   FRAIL CUSTOMER
>   <u>The images are no good!</u>

>   PURVEYOR
>   Get outta here.

>   FRAIL CUSTOMER
>   The images don't hold! You're diluting the images!

She pushes aside Customer; spots Tully, approaches with bagful of colorful cassettes.

>   PURVEYOR
>   Help you out today?

>   WOIWODE
>   No thanks . . .

>   PURVEYOR
>   (rummaging in bag)
>   Got some Kung fu . . . Johnny Carson . . .
>   bloopers from 'Church Windows'—
>   (as Woiwode moves on)
>   How about holotropics: Fugu, just flown in. Got
>   Mimezine . . . Imagithol—

>   WOIWODE
>   Not today.

>   PURVEYOR
>   You're the painter, right? Sorry to hear about your
>   friend. <u>Awful</u> what happened; we're seeing more
>   and more of that—they call it 'image sickness.'

>   WOIWODE
>   I don't approve of drug dealers—I don't even like
>   the way you <u>smell.</u> Save the condolences . . .

>   PURVEYOR
>   You know, I've been looking for you—

>   WOIWODE
>   Get outta my face!

(CONTINUED)

                              PURVEYOR
You have friends in high places. They heard about
your loss; they made something for you—to get
you through the night.

She pulls a cassette out, hands it to him. There's a photo of Tommy
taped across it.

                              PURVEYOR
Come inside—I'll play it for you.

He hesitates a beat. She holds tent flap open; Woiwode enters. The
Purveyor smiles to herself, follows him in.

                                        DISSOLVE TO:

INT. WILD PALMS—BEDROOM—NIGHT

Darkness. A holo ANCHORMAN stands at the foot of the bed.

                              ANCHORMAN
. . . continuing violence in the wake of today's
allegations of doctored holotapes and conspiracy.
A Channel Three engineer has been arrested in
the bizarre case and Harry Wyckoff, the
disgruntled head-of-business-affairs-turned-
revolutionary, is now being sought in the murder
of his wife. Only one week ago, the nation was
shocked when 'Church Windows' was interrupted
by—

CLOSE ON HAND

Its finger presses button on remote control.

BACK TO SCENE

The Anchorman vanishes, replaced by the Harry/Grace murder
holo—it plays eerily MOS. We slowly PAN TO bed. Josie and Tobias
Schenkl are under the covers, intertwined; Josie smokes, muses.

                              TOBIAS
Did you know the entire universe began as a tiny
little speck:
                    (kisses neck)
infinitely hot . . .

                              JOSIE
Infinitely dense. You know, I'm worried about my
brother.

                              TOBIAS
Emotionally?

                                        (CONTINUED)

> JOSIE
> Physically—I talked to the doctors. What if his
> body rejects the chip, Tobias? What if it kills him?

> TOBIAS
> And it was all the 'emperor's New Mind'?
> (shakes his head)
> Not gonna happen. You know your brother,
> Josie—he hasn't come all this way just to let a
> little thing like the <u>body</u> get in his way.
> (beat)
> What will the Senator be like—after the
> transference?

> JOSIE
> Ghostly: When he speaks, it will be like the sound
> the palms make when the leaves clash against
> themselves in the wind.

> TOBIAS
> He'll look like himself?

> JOSIE
> Like a hologram. He'll be able to reach into our
> dreams—by then, half the world will be on
> Mimezine. He'll be like Christ.

They begin to kiss. A KNOCK at the bedroom door; Tobias gets up to answer. Josie's angry at the interruption.

> JOSIE
> This better be good!

Tobias confers sotto voce with a servant.

> TOBIAS
> It's Mr. Wyckoff, in the library—on the
> holophone.

Josie bustles out of bed.

LIBRARY

Harry's image (he's a hologram) sits facing Josie as she enters in robe. As Josie sits, the holophone tracks her with its multi-colored beam. After a beat, Tobias enters wearing one of the Senator's sulkas. He stands in doorframe throughout scene, out of Harry's view.

> JOSIE
> Well, well—if it isn't 'America's Most Wanted.'

> HARRY
> I wanted to tell you that you did a helluva job
> with that tape of me and Grace.

(CONTINUED)

>   JOSIE
> I knew you'd appreciate it.

>   HARRY
> The TV programmer in me screams, <u>this could be</u>
> <u>a hit</u>! Kill a 'mystery' guest off every week. Start
> historically: one week <u>Caesar,</u> the next, <u>Hoffa</u>—

>   HARRY
> 'Death to New Realism! Long live the Friends!'
> Who wrote that dialogue? Did you really think
> anyone would believe it?

>   JOSIE
> Does it matter? We're already climbing up in the
> polls again. Don't you get it? <u>No one gives a</u>
> <u>damn.</u>

>   HARRY
> I want my daughter back, Josie. Does the Senator
> still want to make a deal?

>   JOSIE
> Do you have the chip?

>   HARRY
> <u>Just tell me where to bring it.</u>

Tobias steps over to Josie, sits down beside her.

>   TOBIAS
> Japantown. Sunday, four o'clock—the Festival of
> Ghosts.

Harry reacts when he sees Tobias.

INT. WILDERZONE—HUNGRY GHOST—SAME TIME

Harry sits in booth—across from him are Josie's and Tobias's holos.

CHOKO tends bar; it's uncrowded. Eli Levitt watches the weird
"holophone" call from his stool.

>   HARRY
> Schenkl! You sick <u>animal</u>!

>   TOBIAS
> Don't 'project' on me, Harry. . . .

>   HARRY
> All those years . . . you used what I told you.
> How many died? If I ever get my hands on you—

                                                    (CONTINUED)

CONTINUED:

Oh, please, Harry—stop the adolescent posturing.

                   JOSIE
Sunday, four o'clock. Ciao!

Josie and Tobias' holos vanish. Harry hangs head in frustrated rage.
Eli Levitt walks over, sits. He removes his wedding band and places it
on the table.

                   HARRY
What's this?

                   ELI
The GO chip—when they took it from your hand,
we embedded it in the coating: the wedding band
Josie gave me. I like the irony.

                   HARRY
Why now, Eli?

                   ELI
Word on the street is someone's going to hit the
Senator—soon.

                   HARRY
                 (takes it)
Talk to your people. I don't want anything to
happen to him—not before I get to Deirdre—

                   ELI
I can't control that.

                   HARRY
You've got to try—

Harry slips the wedding band onto his ring finger—he now wears
two bands there. Harry clutches his head, wincing with pain.

                   ELI
What is it?

Harry tilts his head back; a deep blue fluid drips from his nose.

                   HARRY
What—

                   ELI
It's the Mimezine—Schenkl must have overdosed
you at the Perceptory. Come on! I still have some
of the antigen. . . .

He lifts Harry from the booth; Choko comes over to help.

                                        (CONTINUED)

INT. WALT WHITMAN PUBLIC LIBRARY—WOIWODE'S ROOM—DAY

CLOSE ON DISCARDED MIMEZINE AMPULES

CAMERA PANS TO Woiwode, in bed. Sitting on the bed's edge is TOMMY (a hologram), shirtless.

> WOIWODE
>
> I sing the body electric . . . How strange—who is that sitting on my bed? It feels like you—smells like you. Is it a horror? To be gotten through the night by something made at MimeCom? Is it a horror. . . .

> TOMMY
> (stands; boyish)
>
> Hey, Tully, come on! Stop painting, will you? We're gonna be late! It's the Fourth of July—they're making bonfires on the beach—

> WOIWODE
> (crying)
>
> If there's a God, forgive me! For I am lonely, and I am blind!

> TOMMY
>
> Hold me. . . .

Woiwode stands, approaches—but as he does, Tommy's holo begins to break up, fading and reappearing.

> WOIWODE
> (confused)
>
> Tommy?

> TOMMY
>
> Hey, Tully, come on! Stop painting, will you? We're gonna be late!

> WOIWODE
> (afraid)
>
> Tommy, don't leave me!

> TOMMY
> (voice warped now)
>
> They're making bonfires on the beach—

> WOIWODE
>
> Tommy!

Tommy vanishes.

INT. THERAPIST'S OFFICE—DAY

(CONTINUED)

Tobias Schenkl enters from hall. A few beats after he's in, Harry takes him from behind, holding him in a headlock while raising the "rhino knife" for Schenkl to see.

> TOBIAS
> Don't do it, Harry!

> HARRY
> Give me a reason, Tobias!

> TOBIAS
> There are still things you need to know—don't do it—

> HARRY
> Everything I need to know is right in my hand. . . .

> TOBIAS
> If you kill me, you'll never see Deirdre again!

Reluctantly, Harry eases his grip. Tobias shakily walks to his desk, sits.

> TOBIAS
> It isn't safe for you to be out and about. If they pick you up . . .

> HARRY
> Nothing's going to happen to me as long as I have the GO chip.

> TOBIAS
> Why don't you lay down on the couch—like old times.

> HARRY
> Tell me what you know about the chip. What will happen when I give it to the Senator?

> TOBIAS
> He will become immortal. . . .

> HARRY
> It's impossible—

> TOBIAS
> Do you know what paradise is, Harry? No longer encumbered by the body, whatever you imagine is made real before you. That's the GO chip—what your father Dex dreamed only about. . . .

> HARRY
> You're insane—all of you!

(CONTINUED)

> TOBIAS
> Too many of us now, Harry: Synthiotics is
> worldwide. We have our enemies, too—they've
> outgrown the Perceptories. When the election is
> over, those who aren't with us, we will
> enslave—in a thousand Manzanars.

Harry gets woozy: his hand goes to his nose—blue fluid. Then he claps his hands to his ears in pain; we hear CHURCH BELLS accompanying his agonies.

> TOBIAS
> What's the matter, Harry? Cat got your mind?

Schenkl starts to laugh; Harry runs from the room. We STAY ON Schenkl.

EXT. STREETS—DAY

TIGHT TRACKING SHOT WITH Harry as he runs wildly, BELLS clamoring. He stops, holds handkerchief to his nose—great blue stains. WIDEN as he stumbles into his car, collapsing.

> FADE OUT.

END OF ACT TWO

ACT THREE

FADE IN:

EXT. WALT WHITMAN PUBLIC LIBRARY—DAY

ESTABLISHING SHOT.

INT. WALT WHITMAN PUBLIC LIBRARY—DAY

CLOSE ON steel tray. Someone drops acupuncture needles in. We
LOOSEN to reveal Harry, laying on futon, a human porcupine;
Choko deftly removes them. Paige ENTERS FRAME.

> PAIGE
>
> You okay?

> HARRY
>
> What happened?

> PAIGE
>
> They found you in the 'Vette, on the street. What
> happened to you?

Harry puts his fingers to his nose, then looks at them to see any
traces of blue.

> HARRY
>
> Just a heavy session with the shrink.

> PAIGE
>
> Choko's been working on you.

> HARRY
> (ironic)
>
> Comforting.
> (hand to head; troubled)
> I heard the bells. . . .

> CHOKO
>
> (JAPANESE)

> HARRY
>
> What'd she say?

> PAIGE
>
> She says, you've got the sickness, but you're not
> gonna die.

> CHOKO
>
> (JAPANESE)

(CONTINUED)

                         PAIGE
        You're stronger than Tommy was. She calls you
        the 'original rhino dreamer.'

                         HARRY
        Terrific. Does the Senator know you're down
        here?

                         PAIGE
        I couldn't stay with him anymore.

                         HARRY
        You didn't happen to bring any of that snake-in-
        the-bottle stuff—

                         CHOKO
        No alcohol!

Choko has removed the last needles; exits with supplies. Harry
caresses Paige's cheek.

                         HARRY
        It's good to see you.

                         PAIGE
                  (notices ring finger)
        Why the double rings?

                         HARRY
        It's a long story.
                  (stands)
        Let's go.

                         PAIGE
        Where?

                         HARRY
        I just wanna see blue sky.

He takes her hand; they exit.

EXT. HOLLYWOOD HILLS—DAY

They've parked in the Corvette on Mulholland, looking out over the
smoggy cityscape.

                         HARRY
        I open my eyes in the morning, and I think: Is
        what I'm seeing real? First thought of the day.
        What's real, Paige? Can you tell me?

> PAIGE
> Deirdre's real. Peter's real.
> (beat)
> We are . . .

He walks to ridge and stares out. She follows.

> HARRY
> Feel like travelling, Paige?

> PAIGE
> Yes.

> HARRY
> We could fly away somewhere—or live in a big
> old house in the mountains. That's what Grace
> always wanted to do.

Paige lowers eyes, deferring to Grace's memory.

> HARRY
> I want to find some Norman Rockwell-type town,
> with maple trees and park benches and a shiny
> red fire engine. A decent place—where people
> still respect reality.

She smiles, puts her arms around him.

EXT. WILDERZONE—BAZAAR—DAY

As he lopes through the stalls, Tully Woiwode looks worn and
haggard—like so many Holoheads who hang around this section of
the Wilderzone.

> PURVEYOR
> Hey, Twenty-Twenty! Back so soon?

> WOIWODE
> I need more tapes.

> PURVEYOR
> You gonna start paying for these things, Twenty-
> Twenty?

> WOIWODE
> I'm strapped today. The next time—

> PURVEYOR
> I'm out of 'Tommy' tapes.

> WOIWODE
> (desperate)
> Don't cut me off! You'll get your money today!

(CONTINUED)

> PURVEYOR
> <u>I said I'm out.</u> Look, a friend of yours came by.
> She might be able to help you. . . .

> WOIWODE
> Who?

> PURVEYOR
> A lady. Said she'd be over at the Mimeplex. I
> think she has some tapes—

Tommy hurriedly exits; the Purveyor slyly watches him go.

> PURVEYOR
> (to self)
> She'll fix you up, Twenty-Twenty. Fix you up real
> good. . . .

EXT. MIMEPLEX-ODEON—DAY

The marquee reads: MIKE RAUCH IN "WILDERZONE COP" RATED
R.

INT. MIMEPLEX-ODEON—DAY

An uncrowded matinee. Instead of a screen, there's a stage where
holograms are projected by tri-colored beams: The image is of a
grungy apartment with adjacent hall. A COP works his way toward
apartment door, holding his gun. SARA, a blond, eighteen-year-old
junkie, cowers on the other side of the door.

> COP
> Sara? It's McMahon! You need help—you can't
> hide in the Wilderzone forever!

He KICKS IN APARTMENT DOOR and enters. Sara runs, but the Cop
tackles her.

> SARA
> Don't hurt me!

> COP
> Where is he, Sara? Where's Rico?

> SARA
> I don't know!

ANGLE ON WOIWODE. In his seat, perspiring—looks around
nervously. Suddenly, Josie leans forward from darkness of aisle
behind him. He's startled.

> JOSIE
> Hello, Tully. Don't panic—I'm not going to hurt
> you.

(CONTINUED)

                              WOIWODE
You—!

                                JOSIE
                    (touching his special glasses)
You really <u>see</u> with those things?

                              WOIWODE
Yes. And with the Mimezine . . .

                                JOSIE
Phenomenal! I'm so glad. I brought some 'Tommy'
tapes for you: <u>very</u> high quality. I thought it was
better I gave them to you myself—that disgusting
girl in the Wilderzone's been diluting the images.
That's why you can only watch them once.

                              WOIWODE
Why are you doing this?

                                JOSIE
I'm making amends.

She hands him a bag of HOLOTAPES; he looks in, but resists.

                                JOSIE
There is something you could do for me. I've been
looking for Eli Levitt—

                              WOIWODE
No!

                                JOSIE
I understand he's preparing to assassinate my
brother. . . .

                              WOIWODE
Don't make me!

                                JOSIE
I love my brother very much—as much as you
love Tommy. . . .

                              WOIWODE
                           (sotto voce)
Might I but live to see thee in my touch, I'd say I
had eyes again. . . .

                                JOSIE
Come on, Tully—Tommy's waiting for you. . . .

She hands him a holotape. He takes it.

INT. WILD PALMS—SENATOR'S BEDROOM—NIGHT

                                                        (CONTINUED)

Winds blow the curtains in. Coty sits on the Senator bed, pleading.

> COTY
> Don't give Deirdre back!

> SENATOR
> I've never seen you like this—

> COTY
> Josie and Tobias—they're going to kill her! Josie
> hates me!

> SENATOR
> I won't let that happen. It'll be all right, son. . . .

> COTY
> It won't! It won't!

Coty lays his heads on the Senator's lap, and cries; Kreutzer strokes his head.

> SENATOR
> All my sons . . . I thought if I put you under the
> same roof, we'd have a dynasty. I made a mess of
> it, didn't I?

> COTY
> Are you really going to the place where
> holograms go?
> (as the Senator nods)
> But you're not going to die?

> SENATOR
> I'll be stronger than ever.

> COTY
> The GO chip's taking you?

> SENATOR
> They'll put it . . .
> (touches the back of his own head)
> here. See: The way you and I—and Josie—look at
> the world . . . is the right way. The only way. I
> carved this house, Wild Palms, out of the sand.
> The people need someone to lead them out of the
> desert to the oasis. We're building a larger house,
> is all—an ark. A place of many mansions; and we
> will have many to serve us.

> COTY
> Will I be able to see you?

> SENATOR
> Of course.

(CONTINUED)

                              COTY
Touch you?

                            SENATOR
                          (sweetly sad)
No.

                              COTY
Will you forget me?

                            SENATOR
Never.

                              COTY
Don't forget to remember, Daddy. Don't forget to
remember me. . . .

The Senator strokes his son's head.

EXT. WILDERZONE—BAZAAR—DAY

Choko and Eli browse through sidewalk bins. A merchant watches
them. Eli hands a strange tangled root to Choko.

                              ELI
Ask him if this can also be used for image
sickness.

As Eli continues to browse, Choko speaks to merchant in strange
tongue. A battered '60s car pulls up—Men in Suits jump out and
grab him, punching him in the gut. He doubles over. Choko turns
and is shot down; the merchant ducks. Eli is dragged to car with
hood over head.

EXT. MUNICIPAL POOL—ENTRANCE—DAY

The battered car pulls up. Eli is dragged to pool area.

SWIMMING POOL AREA

The pool's filling up—water gushes in from its sides. They sit Eli
down and take off his hood.

                            JOSIE
I've been searching for you.

                              ELI
Shotgun wedding, Josie?

                            JOSIE
More a 'baptism.' Know who told me where to
find you? Your old artist-in-arms—Tully Woiwode.

                                                    (CONTINUED)

                              ELI
              I don't believe that.

                             JOSIE
              Scout's honor. Called me up, all by himself. Even
              told me about the GO chip—hidden in the
              engagement ring I gave you. Is nothing sacred, Eli?

                              ELI
              You won't win, Josie.

                             JOSIE
              Hungry, Eli? You'll love the food here—soup's a
              little watery. . . .

She indicates the pool: Floating in the deep end are a table and
chairs—the ones they sat in the day Eli bit her lip.

                              ELI
              You're sick. . . .

                             JOSIE
              You don't think I'd let you kill my brother, did
              you?
                          (to men)
              Show Mr. Levitt to his table.

Two men in swimsuits drag Eli over to the edge and throw him in,
then jump after. Eli clings to side of pool, with the men in swimsuits
holding him on either side. Josie kneels down close to her old lover.

                             JOSIE
              The revolution's over, Eli. We went in the tunnels
              today and rounded 'em up. They're all
              dead—Harry . . . Deirdre . . . that slut Paige
              Katz—everyone. All your close, personal
              Friends—

Eli reacts painfully to her lies. She nods to the men in swimsuits; they
dunk Eli, then pull his gasping head from the water.

                              ELI
              I'll see you in Hell, Josie—

                             JOSIE
              I was going to suggest some wine, but I don't
              think it's a good idea—one should never drink
              and drown. And you are the designated
              drowner—

She shoves his head under the water and holds it there.

                              JOSIE
            Good-bye, Eli. It could have been so good with
            us.
                     (closing her eyes, almost rapturously)
            So good . . . So good—

INT. WALT WHITMAN PUBLIC LIBRARY—COMMUNAL AREA—DAY

Harry removes the rhino knife from its box and slips it into a sheath at her waist. Paige enters, holding a poster in her hand—of Harry's face, with "INNOCENT" slashed over it. She shows it to him.

                              PAIGE
            They went up overnight—thousands of them.

                              HARRY
            Start the revolution without me.

                              PAIGE
            What time is the rendezvous?

                              HARRY
            Four.

                              PAIGE
            I want to come, Harry.

                              HARRY
            No—

                              PAIGE
            I'm still the Senator's wife—the Fathers are less
            likely to pull anything if I'm there. . . .

                              HARRY
            Have you seen Eli?
                     (as she shakes her head)
            He's the one who's going to kill Kreutzer. If he
            dies before I get to Deirdre . . .

EXT. FESTIVAL OF GHOSTS—DAY

Harry and Paige arrive at colorful "o-bon" festival—dancers, revelers in kimonos, etc.

In a different section of the festival, three Range Rovers pull up. Men in Suits emerge, followed by Deirdre.

Harry and Paige move through crowd. Harry sees Deirdre in distance. As he and Paige move toward her, a procession passes. Paige and Harry get separated by dancers; a Lady Dancer breaks off, following Harry. . . .

                                              (CONTINUED)

The Lady Dancer yanks Harry around a corner, pummelling and wrestling him to the ground. Harry tears off the Dancer's wig, smearing the white-face—it's Tobias Schenkl. Harry pounds the living crap out of him, but Schenkl manages to hang on, getting some licks in.

Paige frantically tries to find Harry. Deirdre stands beside Range Rover, holding onto hand of one of the Men in Suits. Another Man in Suit looks at his watch.

Harry's getting the best of Tobias Schenkl, when Men in Suits appear to rescue the shrink: They knock Harry down and spirit him off. TRACK with Schenkl as they reach the Rover.

>   TOBIAS
>   Let's go!

>   MAN IN SUIT
>   Do we leave the girl?

>   TOBIAS
>   No—change in plans! Move! I said move!

Deirdre's bundled back inside—Harry charges from b.g. The Rovers—and Deirdre—pull away. Harry pounds on the window, where he and Deirdre lock eyes; he's thrown off as the car accelerates. Paige runs up.

>   PAIGE
>   Are you okay?

>   HARRY
>   Yeah. I'm okay.

Harry gets himself together. Paige takes his hands in hers, examining the bloodied knuckles.

>   PAIGE
>   You're bleeding—

>   HARRY
>   (noting hand)
>   The ring—

>   PAIGE
>   What is it?

>   HARRY
>   Eli's ring—they took the ring. It had the GO
>   chip. . . . They took the chip!

>   FADE OUT.

END OF ACT THREE

ACT FOUR

FADE IN:

EXT. STREETS—DAY

Chaos in the streets. Men in Suits clash with Friends as the incident is filmed by rogue cameramen.

> PROTESTERS (V.O.)
> The whole world is watching! The whole world is dreaming! The whole world is watching! The whole world is dreaming!

INT. WALT WHITMAN PUBLIC LIBRARY—DAY

We can hear the PROTESTERS' VOICES in b.g. as Harry and Paige confab.

> PAIGE
> Eli's dead. They've called a War Meeting at MacArthur Park; they're going to attack Channel Three and the lab at MimeCom.

> HARRY
> Where's the Senator?

> PAIGE
> There's a surgical suite at Wild Palms—that's where they did the procedure. . . .

> HARRY
> I'm going—to get Deirdre. I'll come back for you and Peter.

> PAIGE
> I've come all this way for you. Don't leave me behind—not now.

> HARRY
> Where's Tully?

> PAIGE
> No one's seen him; we're worried he was picked up.

EXT. WILDERZONE—BAZAAR—DAY

We START ON "INNOCENT" POSTERS of Harry Wyckoff glued to wall. Tully Woiwode ENTERS FRAME, walks along—jittery and paranoid. He's in withdrawal.

(CONTINUED)

Suddenly, he's grabbed by Floating World boathands and yanked into an alley.

ALLEY

Coty is there, in his maritime captain's outfit, surrounded by Acolytes.

>   COTY
>   Hello, Tully. Been a long time.
>   (beat)
>   You're probably not feeling so good about
>   yourself—after what they did to Eli. . . .

>   WOIWODE
>   I am asking you to kill me. I saved your father's
>   life once—now you can cash me out.

>   COTY
>   This isn't Vegas, Tully!

>   WOIWODE
>   Eli Levitt was my friend! I can barely stay inside
>   my own skin. I am lower than the lowest of
>   animals.

>   COTY
>   You want redemption for what you did. Don't
>   you?

Woiwode starts to cry; Coty tenderly strokes his head.

>   COTY
>   There is a way—to pay back the woman who did
>   this to you. You'd like that, wouldn't you?

Woiwode nods, sobs. Coty snaps his fingers at an Acolyte, who bends down, ear to Coty's lips.

>   COTY
>   You know what to do. Now get me to the
>   chopper; take me to Wild Palms. My sister's
>   waiting for me. . . .

INT. JOSIE'S CONDO—LIVING ROOM—DAY

Schenkl is on the phone. Josie sits on the couch, in darkness, drink in hand. She watches a holo ANCHORWOMAN.

>   ANCHORWOMAN
>   . . . On this day before the election, signs the
>   campaign of Senator Tony Kreutzer is crumbling
>   as support grows for the fugitive Harry Wyckoff.
>   (MORE)

                                                    (CONTINUED)

ANCHORWOMAN (CONT'D)
Wyckoff released copies of his late wife's diaries
to the media earlier today—diaries which support
growing allegations of murder, torture and New
Realist mind control in corridors of MimeCom.
Sporadic violence continues. . . .

TOBIAS
(into phone)
Yes, we'll come. Right away.

He hangs up.

JOSIE
What is it?

TOBIAS
Your brother underwent the procedure.

JOSIE
He was supposed to wait for me—I wanted to be
there!

TOBIAS
Something went wrong. It seems Harry got the
chip to the boy—Peter. He tampered with it;
Chickie taught him some tricks.

The DOORBELL RINGS; Schenkl goes to answer.

JOSIE
(stands, stricken)
I have to go to him!

It's Lt. Grindrod at the door. Before Schenkl can greet him, Grindrod
is shoved inside by a couple of Floating World boathand/acolytes.
They grab Josie and Schenkl. Lt. Grindrod breaks free, makes a move;
they blow him away. Tully Woiwode enters front door. When Josie
sees him, she's terrified.

TOBIAS
You blind fool—what do you think you're doing?

The acolytes pummel Schenkl in the stomach. He falls to the ground;
they kick him as Josie watches helplessly.

JOSIE
Tully, please—

WOIWODE
What a strange world. So dramatic—so . . .
predatory.

(CONTINUED)

                    JOSIE
Don't kill me! Not now—

                    WOIWODE
                    (ironic)
Just when everything was going so well?

                    JOSIE
                    (groping)
Tully—we're like two old generals!

                    WOIWODE
Yin and yang—jewel and lotus!

                    JOSIE
I respect you! Please, Tully! Tell me what you
want!

                    WOIWODE
Once, I was a painter. Mixing colors together was
an . . . ecstasy. I lived for light. Then one day a
woman tore the eyes from my skull.

                    JOSIE
I can give you things—with new technology!
Things you can't imagine—beyond seeing—

                    WOIWODE
Once, I was a painter. Then, my beloved Mazie
was dead.

He puts his hands on her face, ominously caressing the area around
her eyes. The acolytes tighten their vicelike grip, holding her up.

                    WOIWODE
Isn't it strange? Everything you could dream of,
right in your grasp.
                    (beat)
It's over.

                    JOSIE
No!

                    WOIWODE
Who would have thought?

Woiwode kisses her on the mouth.

                    JOSIE
                    (stolid; resigned)
Do it.

Josie screams as he SHOOTS her, then turns the GUN on himself.
Smiles—then pulls the trigger.

(CONTINUED)

INT. WILD PALMS—ENTRY/DEN—DAY

Harry and Paige enter—the place is weirdly silent, deserted. No guards; nothing.

> PAIGE
> I don't like this, Harry. . . .

They enter the den, cautiously. An eerie stillness.

> SENATOR (O.S.)
> Harry? Is that you?

Harry sees the Senator, sitting at his desk, shrouded in darkness.

> HARRY
> Yes, Senator. It's me. . . .

> SENATOR
> I knew you were coming—that's why I sent them all away. This is Mt. Olympus now: Mortals will not be tolerated. I've made an exception—for you.

> PAIGE
> (behind Harry, whispering)
> Something's wrong with him.

> SENATOR
> Some hours ago, I received the GO chip implant. . . .

> HARRY
> How do you feel?

> SENATOR
> They said it couldn't be done. 'Do not pass 'go',' they said.
> (laughs)
> 'Do not collect $200'—

> HARRY
> I want to talk.

> SENATOR
> We never talked enough. That was my fault. Now we have all the time in the world. . . .

> HARRY
> You had more that just an affair with my mother—didn't you?

(CONTINUED)

> SENATOR
> We enjoyed each other's company, Berenice and
> I—Dex wasn't too thrilled. We had a child
> together, did you know? Dex thought it was his.
> Named the boy 'Harry.' He found out, Dex did,
> tried to kill me. I had to defend myself. . . .

> HARRY
> Why didn't you tell me? Instead of this insane
> charade—why?

> SENATOR
> The garden is filled with lies, Harry—little
> lies—thousands over a lifetime, like lilies of the
> field. My lies are MimeCom's—state-of-the-art, for
> the masses. . . .

> HARRY
> You took Peter—my son—away from me. You
> took everything from me I loved. Tell me why!

> SENATOR
> Do you know what the unicorn does when it's
> surrounded by hunters, Harry?

> HARRY
> Tell me why, you psychotic sonofabitch!

> SENATOR
> It somersaults into the nearest abyss, breaking the
> fall with its horn. . . .

Harry's come up close to the Senator now.

> HARRY
> You destroyed Coty—

> SENATOR
> Your brother Coty—it's rather like an Arabian tale,
> isn't it, Harry?

> HARRY
> You made him into a monster—

The Senator's image begins to waffle—we realize he is a holo.

> PAIGE
> Oh my God.

> SENATOR
> (weirdly calm)
> What's happening?

(CONTINUED)

                    HARRY
         We altered the chip—Peter and I. My son . . .
         some of your own people helped us.

The Senator laughs ruefully.

                    SENATOR
         You know, if there was time, I'd tell you all about
         your mother and me. I'd tell you things only the
         wild palms know. . . . Can't feel my legs—ain't
         that the craziest thing?
                    (softly sings)
         Hello, I must be going . . . I cannot stay, I came
         to say, I must be going—

                    HARRY
         Don't leave—not yet! Face me, Father!

                    SENATOR
         I'm glad I came but just the same I must be
         going—

                    HARRY
         You ruined everything you touched. What was the
         matter? Wasn't this world enough?

                    SENATOR
         I'll stay a week or two—

                    HARRY
         You didn't have to run to Paradise—Paradise was
         here! Here, damn you! Paradise was here!

The Senator reaches out for Harry, tenderly. He is waffling and
breaking up now—not much time left.

                    SENATOR
         —but I am telling you, I must be going!

                    HARRY
         Coward!

                    SENATOR
                    (stops singing)
         This is the way the world ends. Not with a bang,
         but a whimp—

He vanishes. Paige sees something outside.

                    PAIGE
         On the terrace!

ANGLE ON DEIRDRE

                                        (CONTINUED)

THROUGH the window, standing on the terrace. Harry and Paige exit.

EXT. WILD PALMS—TERRACE—DAY

Harry rushes to Deirdre—before he can get to her, Coty and several (MARITIME) acolytes emerge from the shadows, with guns. They pull Deirdre back. Coty looks drained.

> COTY
> Did you speak to Father?

> HARRY
> In the living room.

> COTY
> Living room? Funny—his body's in the guest house. You know, I talked to him awhile; then he floated over the roof like a Chagall. . . .

> HARRY
> It's over now.

> COTY
> (laughs weirdly)
> Easy for you to say. Hello, Mother.

> PAIGE
> Let us go.

> COTY
> You're very James Bond today, Mother.
> (to Harry)
> She was always in awe of Pussy Galore. . . .

Harry advances on him. Coty pulls a derringer from his coat.

> COTY
> Stay away!

> HARRY
> All this time, and I find out we're brothers. . . .

> COTY
> (sardonic)
> Harry Wyckoff, this is your life!

> HARRY
> Our father is dead; I'm taking Deirdre. Why don't you come with us? Leave all this behind—

> COTY
> That's what Daddy wanted—to leave everything behind. And look what happened. . . .

(CONTINUED)

                    HARRY
Put down the gun.

                    COTY
Am I going to die old, Harry? Or will I have a
second childhood?

                    PAIGE
Coty, put it down!

                    COTY
                    (shaking head)
Too late . . .

                    HARRY
It was too late for the Senator—not for you. You're
just a boy. . . .

Peter enters.

                    COTY
It's Little Boy Blue!

                    HARRY
Peter, stay back.

                    PETER
I wanted to be here. . . . I belong with you and
Deirdre.

                    COTY
What a poignant moment . . .

                    HARRY
What are you gonna do, Coty? Kill us all?
                    (walks closer; as Coty gets nervous)
Deirdre's watching—what do you think she sees?
The great child guru of Synthiotics? Do you think
she wants to stay with someone like you?

                    COTY
She loves me!

                    HARRY
How could she love a monster?

                    COTY
Don't you talk to me that way!

                    HARRY
Deirdre baby, come on. Come to Daddy. . . .

                    COTY
Leave her alone!

                                        (CONTINUED)

PAIGE
Forgive me, Coty! I closed my eyes to what they
were doing to you!

COTY
(to Paige)
You shut up!

HARRY
If you love Deirdre so much, let her decide for
herself.

COTY
She wants to stay with me! She loves me! I know
she does!

HARRY
Come on, baby. Daddy's here.

COTY
(aimed at Harry)
I'll shoot!

HARRY
In front of your baby sister? You're a lousy role
model, know that?

PAIGE
I'm sorry, baby, for letting them destroy you. I'm
so sorry!

COTY
(spacing out)
I'm the only one now . . . the only Father—

HARRY
(to Deirdre)
Come to Daddy, baby. . . .

PAIGE
(moving toward Coty)
My poor baby!

COTY
(snapping out of reverie)
I'll kill you dead, Mama!

PAIGE
You wouldn't hurt me—give me the gun. . . .

She's almost upon him; Coty hesitates.

COTY
Mother? Who am I?

                                    PETER
                    Father, look out!

One of the Acolytes is about to shoot; Harry wheels on him, FIRING.
The Acolyte gets a SHOT OFF, wounding Paige—as others reach for
guns, Harry finishes them off. Paige has charged Coty, taking gun; he
flees. Suddenly, a piercing scream:

                                    DEIRDRE
                    Daddy!

Deirdre runs to Harry; Peter joins them. All hug, then Harry goes to
Paige, who has a flesh wound. He gathers them up and they exit.

EXT. MIMECOM—NIGHT

The laboratory sign is illuminated by flames.

EXT. ELECTION HEADQUARTERS—NIGHT

CLOSE ON burning campaign poster—a photo of the Senator and
Josie, curling up as it burns, THROUGH shattered window.

EXT. CHURCH OF SYNTHIOTICS—CLOSE ON SIGN—NIGHT

Burning.

INT. CHURCH OF SYNTHIOTICS—NIGHT

Candlelight. Inside, we TRACK PAST a few tattered, frightened
Acolytes, standing before Coty. He is in sooty, tattered robes.

                                    COTY
                    Poor men have grown to be rich men,
                    And rich men grown to be poor again.

                                    ALL
                    And I am running to Paradise.

                                    COTY
                    The wind is old and still at play, while I must
                    hurry upon my way . . .

                                    ALL
                    For I am running—

A burning beam falls and the Acolytes scatter. We PUSH IN ON
Coty, left standing there alone, pathetic. He lifts his head to the sky
with a horrific, rage-filled scream.

EXT. WILD PALMS—ZEN GARDEN—NIGHT

GUNFIRE in b.g. as house is under siege. Someone pours kerosene
onto garden and sets it ablaze. SIRENS KEEN and WAIL in b.g. as we

                                                        (CONTINUED)

PAN UP TO palm tree, its fronds on fire.

EXT. WALT WHITMAN PUBLIC LIBRARY—DAWN

CLOSE ON giant poster of Harry. WE PAN DOWN TO Harry, exiting building with Peter, Paige and Deidre; the Corvette awaits them. Paige's arm is bandaged, spotted with blood. Debris in the streets; triumphant MARCHERS walk arm-in-arm, holding candles.

>   MARCHERS
>   O Captain! My Captain! Our fearful trip is done.
>   The ship has weather'd every rack, the prize we
>   sought is won.

They pull away.

>   PAIGE
>   Where will we go?

>   HARRY
>   I'm taking you to the tunnels at the beach—where
>   Chickie lived. It'll be safe there; I want you to be
>   with the children.

>   PAIGE
>   What will you do?

>   HARRY
>   I have to come back—they need me. Remember
>   what you told me, Paige, about a thousand years
>   ago? That you wanted a world where you could
>   keep your dreams open at night?

Suddenly, a CLANGING of CHURCH BELLS. Harry instinctively touches his nose, checking for "blue" blood—nothing. Then, Harry slows, looks up, over his shoulder—they're passing a church.

ANGLE ON BELLS in tower, RINGING furiously.

Relieved, Harry smiles ironically.

>   HARRY
>   (to self, aloud)
>   O Captain! My Captain! Rise up and hear the
>   bells . . .

He then rockets off. We PAN TO Tobias Schenkl—a ruined man. He watches them go.

>   TOBIAS
>   (re: Harry)
>   You will be my last patient of the day. . . . I will
>   tear your mind apart with my hands—

EXT. PACIFIC OCEAN HIGHWAY—DAY

Harry, Paige, Deirdre and Peter drive along the deserted highway. Peter's in backseat, asleep; Deirdre sleeps in Paige's arms. Harry reaches over and caresses Peter; then strokes Deirdre's head. She stirs.

> HARRY
> (to Paige)
> She talked back there, did you hear her?
> (to Deirdre)
> You're safe now. . . .

She opens her eyes, a little disoriented.

> DEIRDRE
> Daddy?

> HARRY
> What is it, baby?

> DEIRDRE
> There's so much I want to tell you.

Harry smiles—as does Paige.

> HARRY
> There'll be time, baby. There'll be lots of time.

The new day dawns as the fugitives make their way to the tunnels. The water burns with sunlight.

> FADE OUT.

THE END